WRITERS AND THEI

ISOBEL ARMSTR(
General Edit

MARGARET DRABBLE

MARGARET DRABBLE

Glenda Leeming

NORTHCOTE

BRITISH
COUNCIL

© Copyright 2006 by Glenda Leeming

First published in 2006 by Northcote House Publishers Ltd, Horndon, Tavistock,
Devon, PL19 9NQ, United Kingdom.
Tel: +44 (0) 1822 810066 Fax: +44 (0) 1822 810034.

British Library Cataloguing-in-Publication Data
A catalogue record for this book is available from the British Library

ISBN 0-7463-1052-8 hardcover
ISBN 0-7463-0984-8 paperback

Typeset by PDQ Typesetting, Newcastle-under-Lyme
Printed and bound in the United Kingdom
by Athenaeum Press Ltd., Gateshead, Tyne & Wear

Contents

Acknowledgement

I wish to acknowledge Margaret Drabble's kindness in giving her time to discuss her work with me.

Biographical Outline

1939	Born Margaret Drabble on 5 June in Sheffield, Yorkshire, England, to John Frederick Drabble, a barrister, and Kathleen Marie Drabble, née Bloor, the second of four children.
1950s	Goes to the Mount School, York, a Quaker boarding school.
1958	Wins a scholarship to Newnham College, Cambridge, to read English Literature.
1961	Graduates with a starred first-class degree in English. Marries Clive Swift, the actor. Begins to work as an actress playing small parts with the Royal Shakespeare Company at Stratford.
1962	*A Summer Bird-Cage* published.
1964	*The Garrick Year* published.
1965	*The Millstone* published.
1966	Gains travel award from the Society of Authors, and spends some time in Paris.
1967	*Jerusalem the Golden* published.
1969	*The Millstone* filmed as *A Touch of Love* (American title *Thank You All Very Much*). *The Waterfall* published.
1971–2	Separates from Clive Swift.
1972	*The Needle's Eye* published.
1974	*Arnold Bennett, a Biography* published.
1975	*The Realms of Gold* published. Divorce from Clive Swift.
1976	Edits *The Genius of Thomas Hardy*.
1977	*The Ice Age* published.
1979	*A Writer's Britain* published.
1979–85	Edits *The Oxford Companion to English Literature*.

1980	*The Middle Ground* published. Drabble awarded the CBE (Companion of the British Empire).
1982	Marries Michael Holroyd, the biographer.
1987	*The Radiant Way* published.
1989	*A Natural Curiosity* published.
1991	*The Gates of Ivory* published.
1995	*Angus Wilson, a Biography* published.
1996	*The Witch of Exmoor* published.
2000	New edition of *The Oxford Companion to English Literature*. *The Peppered Moth* published.
2002	*The Seven Sisters* published.
2004	*The Red Queen* published.

Abbreviations and References

GI	*The Gates of Ivory* (1991)
GY	*The Garrick Year* (1964)
IA	*The Ice Age* (1977)
JG	*Jerusalem the Golden* (1967)
M	*The Millstone* (1965)
MG	*The Middle Ground* (1980)
NC	*A Natural Curiosity* (1989)
NE	*The Needle's Eye* (1972)
PM	*The Peppered Moth* (2000)
RG	*The Realms of Gold* (1975)
RW	*The Radiant Way* (1987)
SBC	*A Summer Bird-Cage* (1962)
SS	*The Seven Sisters* (2002)
W	*The Waterfall* (1969)
WE	*The Witch of Exmoor* (1996)

(Page numbers with these abbreviations refer to the Penguin editions of Drabble's work.)

AB   *Arnold Bennett, a Biography* (London: Futura Publications, 1975; first published by Weidenfeld & Nicolson, 1974)

1

Margaret Drabble: Career and Critics

Margaret Drabble became famous in the 1960s for her short novels about young women starting life, but she has grown into a much more powerful and interesting novelist through the years into the twenty-first century. The early novels of the sixties coincided with the growth of the Women's Movement, and the preoccupations of the graduate wife and the working mother; they thus first attracted the attention of feminist critics. By 1989, however, Margaret Drabble was saying '*The Radiant Way* is not a woman's book, it's about the decline of western civilisation',[1] an expansion of subject matter that alienated some of her critics, who stubbornly continued to search her work for female role models and patriarchal oppression. Both feminist themes and social critiques, related as they in any case are, arose from Drabble's own experience. Born in 1939, the second of four children of two first-generation Cambridge graduates (her older sister is A. S. Byatt, the novelist), she grew up during war-time and vividly remembers post-war austerity, when expectations were low and simple luxuries were highly appreciated. Margaret Drabble says 'I think it's absolutely wonderful to be able to buy a bag of bananas – but this is the war-baby thing – that one is grateful for small mercies. A lot of people aren't'.[2]

Because Drabble's parents had struggled to get to Cambridge at a time when it was much more difficult for working- or lower-middle-class students, they were determined that their children should secure the same advantage; as a reasonably successful barrister, John Drabble was able to send all four children to good, single-sex Quaker boarding schools, from which they went on to Cambridge: Margaret Drabble read English

Literature at Newnham, and got a starred first-class degree, the best possible result for an undergraduate, and her reading has informed her writing more perhaps than most other novelists of the period.[3] Immediately she graduated, she married Clive Swift, the actor, who was by now working for the Royal Shakespeare Company at Stratford. Drabble, who had acted in student productions, was anxious to become an actress, and joined her husband in Stratford, where she eventually got small parts and understudying (curiously, however, she dislikes writing plays and does not wish to speak about the ones she has written[4]). Adjusting to marriage was not made any easier by her becoming pregnant soon afterwards, but during her pregnancy, as acting became impractical, she began to write her first novel, *A Summer Bird-Cage*, in 1962.

This and the next few novels tend to explore women's experience with some relationship to Margaret Drabble's own life: she had already married when she wrote about Sarah, her first heroine, who is a young woman still hovering on the brink of marriage. By the time she wrote *The Garrick Year* (1965), about a mother of two small children, Drabble had two children herself and was about to have a third. *The Millstone* then returns to the experiences of first pregnancy and childbirth, by which time Drabble is a mother of three. She also experienced the strains of a less than ideal marriage, as Clive Swift was often away in productions and, unlike her heroine Emma, Drabble did not usually go with him – 'I didn't go up and down to Stratford, I stayed in London'.[5] In 1966 she received a travel award by the Society of Authors, and recalls 'My husband was in the theatre in Chichester, and I suppose that was really the parting of the ways in a sense, because I decided "He's not going to come with me and I'm damned if I'm turning it down, simply because he's not going to come with me. I'll go!"' And she took the children with her to live in Paris for a while.[6]

By the time she wrote *The Needle's Eye*, about the divorced reluctant celebrity Rose, Drabble's own marriage was deteriorating, and by 1972 she had separated from Clive Swift, remaining a single parent for the next decade, writing about a series of women in the same situation.

By taking such topics – early marriage; the shock of domesticity for the working or intellectual woman; the impact of babies on parental lifestyle, especially in upsetting established priorities and self-image; failing marriage – Drabble's first few novels spoke directly to her generation, especially to women. These problems were being aired more vigorously throughout the sixties as Drabble's war-baby generation and the baby-boomers of the late forties and early fifties reached adulthood. Full employment, rising wages, improved technology and more entertainment changed the conditions of their adolescence. Naturally women as well as men no longer accepted the obligation of ceaseless toil, in the workplace or at home. So it was not only privileged graduates who recoiled from the traditional patterns of marriage and the family: as the norms of youth culture spread into all classes and regions of Britain, young women of various backgrounds were interested in the changing shape of marriage and of women's expectations in society.

Drabble has mentioned that feminist issues were what her readers wrote to her about,[7] and Dee Preussner, for instance, points to the novels as showing 'the ways that one can build a self'.[8] But the very factor that made Drabble's novels attractive both to the novel-reading public and to the academic establishment also led to unease with her work; the sense that she was, like several of her characters, 'an intellectual wolf in middlebrow sheep's clothing' as Valerie Grosvenor Myer put it,[9] produced dissatisfaction with her lack of overt commitment to the feminist cause. Lynn Veach Sadler's study sees Drabble as 'saccharine when she talks about children'[10] and the 'Drabble Woman' as an incoherent mixture of 'the real thing, cultivating one's garden, aureate imagery, inconclusiveness, cuteness of style, emphasis on the past, succouring the unlovely, solipsism, privilege, grace, fate, chance, and luck'.[11] By 1995, Jita Tuzyline Allan condemned *The Middle Ground* as creating 'a psychic landscape populated by self-doubting, emotionally crippled women', women who are 'less content and much more neurotic' than Virginia Woolf's heroines,[12] while 'Drabble's early fiction sets the tone of an unmitigated sexual determinism ... in spite of a successful feminist movement'.[13]

Margaret Drabble pointed out that she had been following her own ideas, without being aware of a feminist ideology,[14] as the Women's Movement was not yet prominent when she

started to write; her views were in fact comparatively conservative, as she took a more individualist position that 'There's
no use pretending that marriage is in a good state ... It's no good
blaming patriarchy of men for this. Both sexes are at fault. And
the institution of marriage itself is at fault'.[15] This moderate
liberal humanist tone became defensive at times, as when
describing the subject matter of *The Middle Ground* just before its
publication, she said 'It is in a way a response to, not so much
feminist criticism as feminist journalism. The novel is about the
change of tone and consciousness. And whether feminism is still
a good cause'.[16]

Drabble's characters have then been criticized for neuroticism, and at the same time were seen as denying their true
problems by the Freudian critic Nicole Suzanne Bokat, who
claims that their subjection to chance and accident shows 'their
inability to take responsibility for their lives ... Margaret Drabble
contends that she embraces a classical [sic] fatalism, therefore
rejecting Freud's concept of psychotherapy'.[17] This judgement
overlooks the variation in Drabble's characters, men as well as
women, many of whom are very interested in deciding what
decisions to take, rather than in acting without reflection.
Drabble herself often refers to Freud, and does not totally
dismiss psychotherapy – her reservations apply only to some
people, 'who should never have a Freudian analysis. Those are
the people who are innately selfish and want to be told it's not
their fault'.[18]

Drabble herself asserts the importance of biographical background in understanding a writer's work, in spite of her
absorption of the New Criticism/Leavisite position that biography, like the author's intention, should be strictly ignored: 'I
was taught not to pay any attention to it, but I find it
increasingly interesting. It's so obvious that writers are
influenced by the way their parents behaved. It seems to me
ridiculous to isolate a text, in fact almost meaningless'.[19] Critics
and interviewers have, however, usually trodden delicately
around the issues of Drabble's tense relationships with her
mother and elder sister, which seem to underlie the series of
vampirish or inadequate mothers and unsympathetic sisters that
her heroines have to contend with. Drabble believes that she
was her mother's favourite,[20] but was perhaps all the more

4

marked by her mother's grim, depressive character: 'she was a highly intelligent, angry, deeply disappointed and manipulative woman' (*PM* 390). Certainly 'monster mothers' appear in many of the novels, oppressing their unfortunate daughters. Closer to home, she noted that although *The Needle's Eye* had reflected her last efforts to keep her marriage together, if she had written it a little later she might have ended it differently, and, instead of sending Rose back to her husband, 'I might have allowed her her freedom'.[21]

Feminist criticism was somewhat dissatisfied with the implications of *The Needle's Eye*, in that its main woman character is given to religious or mystical self abnegation, and even returns to an abusive ex-husband. Its predecessor *The Waterfall* had presented somewhat ambiguously a passionate traditional love affair in which the heroine submerges her own personality in this love. With *The Needle's Eye*, in fact, having experimented with alternating and contradictory viewpoints in the very narrowly focused *Waterfall*, Drabble was widening her field to take in a broader range of situations and social levels. While Allan implies disingenuousness in attitudes towards Drabble's expansion of subject matter – 'Drabble in effect is being praised for moving from the petty subject of nature (women) to the weightier one of culture (men)'[22] – the later novels place both men and women in relation to each other within culture, and if the subject matter sometimes includes 'the breakdown of western civilisation', women's role as instrument and/or victim is often to the fore. Some readers' reactions to these two novels made Drabble uneasy, and she said of *The Waterfall*: 'I've been attacked really very seriously and I can only respect the attack by people who say that you should not put into people's heads the idea that one can be saved from fairly pathological conditions by loving a man. People say that's not how I can approach my life. There's no guidance in that for me. And that's true'.[23]

At intervals during her novel-writing, Drabble wrote short stories for various magazines, not as yet collected. There is no space to discuss these in detail, but naturally similar themes and motifs appear in the stories, and one might mention the early 'Hassan's Tower', where the narrator establishes a tolerant attitude to his new wife Chloe, something like Simon's towards Julie, and 'Crossing the Alps', where the misfortunes that afflict the holiday of a pair of adulterous lovers is reminiscent of *The Waterfall,* and the narrative description of their delicate and hopeless relationship unfolds in long, Jamesian sentences as do parts of *The Needle's Eye.* There is also a story called 'Homework' where the main character is like Kate in *The Middle Ground,* and is driven beyond endurance by a burdensome acquaintance, as Kate is by her irksome suitors; the tactless acquaintance is the strongly unreliable narrator, an ironic approach Drabble has not cared to pursue throughout a long novel.

Margaret Drabble has explained in several interviews that her childhood and adolescence was influenced by the work ethic of her family background and by the public service ethic of her Quaker boarding school.[24] Her interest in moral issues was encouraged by the ideology of the English faculty at Cambridge (she summarizes the Leavisite view that a novel should 'engage with serious subjects', should 'enact its moral meaning' and should not be playful[25]) so the treatment of the moral dilemmas of individual young women gradually expands to include wider social and personal pressures.

The much admired *The Realms of Gold* was greeted with acclaim as returning to the central concerns of the working single parent, the energetic Frances Wingate being seen as a role model for modern women. It can, however, also be regarded as developing *The Needle's Eye'*s concern with social trends, moving from London to the provincial Midlands, juxtaposing the diverse lives of her varied characters.

The Ice Age even more forcefully establishes Drabble's interests in the 'condition of England' in the seventies, and, like *The Needle's Eye,* focuses on a male character as protagonist, but sketches in a broad picture of the economic and social crises affecting Britain at that time. Her dislike of the culture of greed which was already beginning to appear in the seventies underlies this novel, and at this point she was already beginning to sit on various committees, in recognition of which she was awarded the CBE in 1980.

The Ice Age is a 'condition of England' novel, and with *The Middle Ground* she produced a 'London novel' which pursued the same anxieties about declining public services, materialism, violence on the streets, and another female protagonist who struggles with her destiny, this time with a mid-life crisis. The emptiness of this phase of existence did not, however, reflect Drabble's own feelings; unlike her protagonist, she had a full and demanding private and professional life: in 1982 she married the well-known biographer Michael Holroyd. At the same time she had embarked on producing a new edition of *The Oxford Companion to English Literature*, a task which took her from 1978 to 1985, and, she says, was exhausting and time-consuming to a degree far exceeding what she was being paid to do – but it had beneficial effects in widening her own awareness of literature and criticism.[26]

In retrospect, Drabble noted that, as far as modern critical theory was concerned, literature graduates of her generation 'lived in ideological terminal naïveté, and I suppose I cherished that naïveté as being somehow creative ... the compiling of *The Oxford Companion to English Literature* during the years 1979–85 put paid to that naïveté for me'[27] – in that it forced her to read articles on literary theory, and contemplate the opportunities they suggested: 'The glittering supermarket of postmodernism ... was suddenly opened to us. We could choose. We could shop around. We could mix and pick'.[28]

The glittering supermarket encouraged Drabble to continue to use a more interventionist narrator, as she had begun to do in *The Realms of Gold*, and to mix time-schemes and narrative forms, as appeared in her next three novels, *The Radiant Way* trilogy. Some newspaper reviewers still see the interventionist narrator as upsetting a desired state of illusion or as coercive or confrontational,[29] but academic critics are more appreciative. Valerie Grosvenor Myer notes that a result of the postmodern slide of narrator from one position to another is that 'readers could no longer easily find or identify with Drabble woman, or find the nuclear family',[30] but this does not mean that the novels are less accessible to the average reader who, at the same time, has also become more sophisticated and accustomed to changes of focus and frame in film and television:

> I am very conscious that my later novels reflect much of this new, speeded-up culture, not always to the satisfaction of the critics and readers. They manifest a perhaps excessive number of story-lines and they cut between them with great rapidity. They are full of sudden breaks, of hops and jumps, of swift changes of focus, of zooms and zaps and other motions drawn from other media. In this

they reflect the world we inhabit and the media we are informed by, but I am not at all sure that I can make the format do what I want it to do.[31]

A further revision of *The Oxford Companion* led to a gap of two years in her productive life: it was possible to do some journalism and minor writing, but not to work creatively on a novel. The next Drabble work was *The Witch of Exmoor*, which she was disappointed to find readers taking too realistically. 'It was meant as a satire, which surely the title ought to have told people – it shows a range of totally selfish middle class people.'[32] After this, changing direction abruptly, Drabble wrote a partly fictionalized version of her parents' biography, focusing on her mother, trying to understand what had made this difficult woman the way that she was. Depressive for much of her life, Marie Drabble had had a strong effect on her children: in the early seventies, Margaret Drabble commented that her mother was now better 'thanks to, well quite frankly, thanks to drugs ... I don't know how I would have developed if I had known my mother as she is now. She is so much more cheerful and active'.[33] In *The Peppered Moth*, however, the tone is harsh; clearly, in spite of repeating that her later relationship with her mother was not conflictual,[34] Drabble finds it hard to define her own feelings: 'I think about my mother a good deal, uncomfortably. Night and day on me she cries' (*PM* 390). Writing this book was demanding and time-consuming, and she found writing her next book, the shorter *The Seven Sisters*, a relief. Perhaps surprisingly, then, she next ventured on another more distant historical reconstruction in *The Red Queen*, where her cautious and spare account of a Korean princess's life contrasts with a dependent tale about a modern reader of the princess's memoirs.

Paradoxically, as Drabble's novels become more experimental and innovative, critics take a less holistic view of her work, seeking out aspects to compare to other novelists, or concentrating on psychological or philosophical themes. My interest is in the way that the narratives reflect the themes and attitudes of the novels, so that, although Drabble says that she does not plan or structure her work in advance, the plots take a certain shape, dependent on Drabble's underlying preoccupations.

2

Narrative Structure in Drabble's Works

Natural curiosity – to find out what and why things happen – is the main reason for reading or listening to a narrative, and a narrative basically is an account of a series of events linked by cause and effect;[1] inasmuch as there is a strong emphasis on cause and effect, this chain of events can also be referred to as plot, another term which has been widely discussed and probed.[2] Traditional narrative theory focuses on the role of the writer in choosing, emphasizing and explaining the rational links between plot events, and more recent critics have stressed the way that the reader accepts, rejects, infers or imagines the links.[3] Margaret Drabble's novels vary in the amount of interpretation required of the reader: even in an early novel like *A Summer Bird-Cage* where the reasons for events are carefully explained, there is still an area of uncertainty for the reader as to the motives of the characters; and conversely, even in the later *The Middle Ground,* which avoids a final solution, some firm and convincing reasons for its characters' behaviour appear.

As the title of *A Natural Curiosity* implies, curiosity about causes is important in revealing the workings of the plot, and the power and limitation of curiosity about causes is probed and explored. 'I want to know *what really happened*' (*NC* 75) says one of the characters in that novel, and the possibility of finding out what and why things happen is a goal to which characters themselves repeatedly address themselves, though often to be frustrated. Margaret Drabble has said:

> What I usually do is take characters who are reassessing how they've got to be what they are, rather than showing, as in a Bennett novel, the time span viewing how they become it. I admire people who can

do the longer time span. But I tend to look back rather than carry them through the course of the book. I find it more interesting for some reason.[4]

This means that cause and effect are foregrounded, as the characters probe into their past, and although it is not true that all Drabble's novels reject forward-moving plots, large parts of most of them are taken up with reminiscences, memories, investigations, family histories and other material that could help to give a clarification of why the character has reached this stage in his or her life.

Nonetheless, as many critics have noticed, it is a feature of Drabble's plots that sudden often horrifying events occur, accidents that have no possible relation to what went before: the chain of cause and effect is supplemented by unpredictable interventions. Drabble points to the inevitability of this:

> That is what is so interesting about life: choosing to be something and being struck down while you do it by a falling brick. The whole question of free will and choice and determinism is inevitably interesting to a novelist. Perhaps I go on about it more than some.[5]

The intervention of accident does not negate this operation of cause and effect in a plot: the accidents themselves may be causeless, but they have a logical influence on the characters and plot events, which are *not* causeless. It may be, as I shall discuss later, that some accidents have surprisingly little effect, and also that apparent causes are questioned and left un-determined, but on the whole the narratives reach backward into the characters' past and into the past of the community for more and more remote causes, asking why characters and society as a whole are as they are.

Accident, the falling brick, is the wild card in the game of 'free will and choice and determinism', potentially supporting the concept of determinism against free will and choice, but also threatening us with a totally random universe. Elsewhere Drabble has suggested that all the apparently random events that bombard the characters may have some kind of reason – that cause and effect are secretly at work, in a deterministic pattern.

> What I'm perpetually trying to work out is the relationship between coincidence and plan. And in fact, I have this deep conviction that if

10

you were to get high up enough over the world, you would see things that look like coincidence are, in fact, part of a pattern. This sounds very mystical and ridiculous, but I don't think it is. I think that I, in particular, and maybe certain other people have a need to perceive this pattern in coincidence. It may be that psychologically we're so afraid of the unpredictable, of the idea of chaos and disorder, that we wish to see order.[6]

Here she is also acknowledging what Freud says, that coincidences are just that, random events, and it is need in the human observer that invests them with significance. As she says,

It's very unlike human beings to believe that things are accidents; they are constantly looking for reasons, aren't they? It's one of the conditions of being human that one is always looking for a cause. And if one can't find a cause in oneself, then one looks for an agent behind that.[7]

Then she also suggests a more 'writerly' role for individuals, not as readers but as directors of their own lives:

Well, we certainly do live in a world of chance, there's no disputing that. The duty of the human will is to seek to make sense of it and to resist being swamped by the arbitrary and saying because it's arbitrary there's nothing you can do. You have to endeavour in the face of the impossible. That's what we were put on this earth to do: to endeavour in the face of the impossible.[8]

Affected as they are by incomprehensible accidents, the characters themselves are all the more anxious to find reasons for their behaviour. Psychological determinism is one of the traditional explanations, but from what does the determining psychology derive? Heredity and environment are anxiously explored in the frequent forays into the past, with parents, environment, upbringing, all examined, the quest for explanation forming a large part of the narrative. Referring to determinism and accident, Drabble remarked, 'The two concepts fit frightfully well together. The accidents are all planned and one's fate is planned. It is going to contain certain accidents. There is nothing you can do about it'.[9]

The 'reassessing how they have got to where they are' aspect of Drabble's novel structures is thus concerned particularly with the individual character's unique experiences and reaction to them, though, as she says in *The Gates of Ivory*, the individual is also only one of huge numbers of similar people undergoing similar pressures and influences, and to pick out one person may falsify the experience of others, though the narrative is true for that one person.

In her more 'naïve' period Drabble, when discussing her work, referred generally to herself as 'the writer', even when proposing an intrusive form of narrator: 'Everybody knows the writer is there – why shouldn't he [sic] say so? It seems very artificial, in a way very pretentious, to pretend that there is no writer, that everything is occurring'.[10] Early theories of narrative divide the responsibility for a text and its meanings along an orderly chain of participants, symmetrically balanced between author, implied author, narrator, narratee, implied reader and actual reader. More recent theorists, however, have suggested that this is both too divisive and too crude: although a first-person narrator is usually easy to distinguish, as a character, from the implied author, as we see with Emma Evans and Jane Gray, for a third-person narrator the relationship is very close, and suggests identification, if the narrator is not obviously a very unreliable one. The line of distinction usually suggested between the two is that the implied author selects, orders and allocates the material of the text, whereas the narrator observes and presents this material through his or her discourse. In some of Margaret Drabble's third-person novels, however, this distinction breaks down, and a more flexible description is needed.

As has often been noticed, she begins to use the third-person narrator unobtrusively in *Jerusalem the Golden* and *The Needle's Eye*, and then develops a more interventionist narrator in the novels from *The Realms of Gold* onwards. What is unusual is that in these interventions the narrator sometimes takes on the role of implied author too, by directly discussing the manipulation of the plot – here, in *The Realms of Gold*, 'I' is the narrator,[11] rejecting her own planned transition between two scenes:

> I had a fine leap, from Janet staring at the small crater in her melted wax candle, to David staring into the crater of a small volcano. It would have been an arbitrary link, but I liked it, and am sorry that I have messed it up by this perhaps unnecessary fit of explanation. The truth is that David was intended to play a much larger role in this narrative, but the more I looked at him, the more incompre-

hensible he became, and I simply have not the nerve to present what I saw in him in the detail I had intended. (*RG* 183–4)

At other points, the narrator comments on the action as if it were existing in the real world, unchangeable, and available only for description and comment. In *The Waterfall*, the first-person narrator says about Gordale Scar (a waterfall over stone cliffs in Yorkshire which actually exists): 'it is real, unlike James and me, it exists. It is an example of the sublime' (*W* 236), and Margaret Drabble later glossed this as meaning that the characters' sublime romantic passion has reality in the real world, even if this example is only fictional; 'this kind of thing', romantic passion, exists and gives a Platonic reality to its fictional vectors, as the narrator would have paraphrased it:

> You may well think that James and I do not exist because we are characters in fiction and this kind of thing happens in fiction all the time and isn't true. But if you think a little more you will realize that we exist. It exists and this could only be a record of true experience. Otherwise why should anybody want to invent it.[12]

Drabble adds 'That's what I meant by it. But I put it in a kind of apologia'. Elsewhere in *The Waterfall* the narrator oscillates between the manipulative, inventing, implied author and the narrating reporter of the truth: she says of her lover James, injured in a car crash, 'I could have maimed James so badly, in this narrative, that I would have been allowed to have him, as Jane Eyre had her blinded Rochester. But I hadn't the heart to do it, I loved him too much, and anyway it wouldn't have been the truth because the truth is that he recovered' (*W* 231). So we have here a narrator who discusses how she is going to manipulate and invent her fictional material, who could be termed the 'organizing narrator', and a narrator who asserts the factual nature of the material described, or 'presenting narrator'. Margaret Drabble herself has no explanation or rationale for the coexistence of these two narrative approaches often within the same novel: she says, 'I don't decide on one day to write in one way and on another day to write in the other way; they just occur'.[13]

Apart from the self-referential comments on the material and its truth status, two further functions of the narrator appear and are the same as those found in many nineteenth-century novels;

that is, the interventions of the narrator, firstly in making authoritative statements (about life, the universe in general), and secondly in addressing the reader in a friendly, or more often challenging, way. Often, in fact, the authority of such statements is mitigated by an ironic tone; Drabble says that one cannot make general statements about such large subjects with real authority in a novel, and so she tries to incorporate an ironic distance. An example appears in *The Middle Ground*, where the authoritative narrator lists things that happen in Great Britain and the world with irony implied in the inappropriately casual, even blasé tone conveyed by 'various other', 'another':

> Hundreds of students shot one another in universities in Turkey, Iraq, Pakistan and various other trouble spots.
> An article in the *New Statesman* argued that the Western view of the veil as a garment of female repression was fundamentally ill-informed and misguided.
> Another corrupt African regime fell, to general rejoicing.
> Sam Goldman's play came off after only twenty-six performances, though Hugo had decided on reflection that it was, after all, quite a memorable work.
> The *New Statesman* acquired a new editor and several of its staff resigned, and the paper for which Kate and Hugo write, teetered on the brink of closure, filling both of them with apprehension and excitement.
> Another Iraqi diplomat was shot in Piccadilly.
> An Irishman claimed to have planted a bomb in Beckton sewage works that would spread disease and destruction for many miles around ... (*MG* 213)

More personal address to the reader varies, such as the insincere propitiation of the narrator of *A Natural Curiosity*, who tells us 'this is not a political novel', continuing, after detailing Alix's obsession with severed heads, 'No, not a political novel, more a pathological novel. A psychotic novel. Sorry about that. It won't happen again. Sorry' (*NC* 193–4). This may contribute to the impression that the narrator, or through the narrator the author, is a communicative presence.

In practice, the use of a personal narrator is important to Margaret Drabble's popularity as a writer. Although Mieke Bal claims that 'narrator or narrative agent' means only 'the linguistic subject, a function and not a person, which expresses itself in the language that constitutes the text',[14] and therefore should be referred to as 'it' rather than 'he' or 'she',[15] it seems fair to say that the vast majority of readers regard a speaking subject as a person, not an 'it', and in spite of greater or lesser awareness of constructedness, will usually see the construction as a person, not a thing. In general Margaret Drabble herself considers that her third-person narrators are very close to herself – 'they are me; they are not unreliable'.[16]

But the confidential tone of many of the Drabble narrators, including the early first-person ones, leads readers to feel complicit and sympathetic to the narrator. Wayne C. Booth suggests that the reader as constructing meaning also needs to take into account personal response, what he calls, 'my irresistible impulse to deal with the text as a person, or, if you prefer, as the act of a person, the implied author'.[17] His view is that 'there is always a game going on between author and reader'.[18] Drabble admitted to writing at first with an eye to pleasing the reader: 'I was possibly afraid of writing dully or alienating an audience. My first novels are much more ingratiating and made more concessions to the reader.'[19] Making concessions in this way is a simpler game that the challenges and conflicts which the later narrators put forward to the reader, and readers who came to enjoy the confidences of the organizing and presenting narrators felt disoriented when the narrator of *The Witch of Exmoor* gave a more aggressive turn to the game.

In looking at Drabble's novels in more detail, then, it is interesting to focus on the management of the narrative material, specifically how the chosen time-scale is interleaved with material from the past; another narrative method for foregrounding certain issues is the juxtaposition of observer characters alongside a series of plot events, whether this observer is a major character in his or her own right, like Sarah (*A Summer Bird-Cage*) or Simon (*The Needle's Eye*) or even a minor outsider figure, like Mujid (*The Middle Ground*). The role of the narrators, fulfilling the various functions, whether organizing, presenting, authoritative or personal, varies within novels as well as between them, and is responsible for the amount of distance that is felt between the reader and the narrative.

3

Spots of Time: Managing a Focused Narrative

It was useful for Drabble's subsequent reputation that *A Summer Bird-Cage* caught the public's imagination, raising issues of female self-assertion and autonomy. This novel was published in 1962: typically of its time, it sees marriage as almost inevitable for a woman (by 1973, in contrast, Frances Wingate in *The Realms of Gold* can hardly contemplate the idea of a two-parent family any longer).

It is worth looking in some detail at this plot, as Drabble wrote it spontaneously and without a plan, 'as if writing a long letter'.[1] The titles of its eleven chapters (which include 'The Wedding', 'The Reception', 'The Invitation', 'The Party', 'The Next Invitation', 'The Next Party') mark the temporal unfolding of the plot, which is in fact very simple. Sarah Bennett, the first-person narrator, is enduring a year in a kind of limbo after leaving university, suffering the double affliction of being unable to decide what to do with her life, and of being separated from her boy friend Francis who is spending the year on a scholarship in America.

The novel begins with her coming to her parents' house to be a bridesmaid, as her beautiful, antagonistic sister Louise is marrying an unlikeable novelist, Stephen Halifax. Over the next few months, Sarah gradually discovers that her sister is – and probably was already – having an affair with John Connell, actor and best man at the wedding. Almost as soon as Sarah pieces all this together, Louise's marriage abruptly ends: Stephen catches her with John and throws her out. Looking back from what must be about six months later, Sarah tells us 'As I sit here, typing these last few pages', that Louise is rather provisionally living

16

with John, and Sarah herself is looking forward to marrying Francis, soon to return as the year is over.

Short though it is, the novel has a double plot, sliding between Sarah and Louise. Marriage, the main theme, is described in the Webster passage from which the title phrase comes (*The White Devil*, Act I scene 2) as like a summer bird-cage, where the birds outside try to get in, and those inside try to get out. Running beneath or parallel to this theme is the topos of the rite of passage: Sarah's task is to make the belated transition from the comparatively protected, structured student life to that of an adult, with its open choices and fewer predeterminations. One of her options is marriage, and thus her fascinated scrutiny of Louise's marriage, among those of her other friends, helps her to make up her mind about her own destiny. The plot, then, reveals Louise's struggles, and at the same time traces Sarah's anxieties and indecision.

Barbara Milton perceptively suggests that many of Drabble's novels included an 'understudy' element – a woman observed and compared herself with another woman – perhaps, she says, related to Drabble's experience of understudying in the theatre at this time?[2] This is, however, a pattern not limited to women, as we see in the Simon–Rose plotting of *The Needle's Eye* and in the Stephen–Liz (and others) dual plot in *The Gates of Ivory*. The variations on this counterpoint pattern have a wider scope in displaying a contrast of two ways of life, for individuals or groups.

In *A Summer Bird-Cage*, then, all the vivid drama of the plot takes place in the intermittently revealed Louise part of the story: the classic triangular relationship of Louise, Stephen and John is conveyed in stages, and Sarah, like a secondary character in a Henry James novel, is mainly confined to observing and discovering. Thus Sarah both is and is not at the centre of the novel, a dual position she recognizes when she says 'I meant to keep myself out of this story, which is a laugh, really, I agree; I see however that in failing to disclose certain facts I make myself out to be some sort of *voyeuse*, and I am too vain to leave anyone with the impression that the lives of others interest me more than my own' (*SBC* 73).

Sarah is in fact well aware of the pitfalls ahead, and struggles to find some shape of marriage that will not lead to a loss of individuality and self-hood on one hand, or constant suffering and conflict on the other. What interests Sarah in Louise's choice is that it is the classic, self-interested marriage for money: she says 'I think you're the only person I know who married for money. I know they're always doing it in books but I thought it was just a novelist's convention' (*SBC* 195).

Sarah then contrasts Louise's mercenary choice with her friend Gill's early marriage for love, which has rapidly degenerated into quarrels, resentment and separation. Though Drabble later says that she avoided schematic plotting – 'when the book remains schematic it's boring'[3] – Sarah's choices here are recognized explicitly: 'I was dimly beginning to formulate the idea that of all the many kinds of marriages, Gill's and Louise's represented some kind of extreme, and that both extremes were to be avoided' (*SBC* 74). This helps Sarah to clarify her own intentions: she rejects the idea that she will be (merely) 'a don's wife' – she says she is going 'to marry a don' (*SBC* 137), meaning that marrying will be only one thing among the many that make up her identity – and these words show that she is highly sensitive to the de-individualizing effects of even a happy marriage, an impression reinforced by her unease at occasional glimpses of her 'cosy' married friend Stephanie, nicely but rapidly sinking into complacency. Unlike other Drabble protagonists, Sarah does not look back much into the past to find out how she got where she is: apart from a few comments on her parents' strained relationship, the survey of her contemporaries' marriages provides the material for her to assess what she really wants.

It had been pointed out that Drabble's novels tended to cover a time span of nine to twelve months, the time it took her to write a novel,[4] but this is not strictly true, as the final paragraphs, indicating that about a year has passed since the events at the beginning of the novel, are a only postscript to the main plot events which end much earlier. The time-scheme is carefully signposted with dates and intervals noted, beginning with Louise's wedding in September, and working towards the climax or catastrophe on 18 December, with parties or invitations more specifically pinned down to 10 November, 7 December and 18 December. The wedding reception introduces John Connell as best man, and at a London party Sarah meets him again, but at that point his angry questions do not make it clear to her whether he is having, has had or has failed to have a relationship with Louise. It is only when she meets Wilfred Smee, a friend of both Stephen and John, at the next party in Louise's flat, that all is revealed (Wilfred Smee seems in fact to be a character whose only function is to transmit information).

The climactic meeting of the two sisters, in which Louise rather unexpectedly asks Sarah to spend the evening with her, appears on the surface not to be well motivated, but is psychologically plausible because, as Louise becomes more involved with John, she loses interest in keeping up appearances as a worldly married socialite, and Sarah comments 'I guessed, from watching them that they needed an audience to build up the striking, wicked image of themselves' (*SBC* 182).

Time is here bunched up rather improbably, as John and Louise are going off to spend the night together at Louise's flat, while her husband is away, and this is the very night when Stephen returns unexpectedly, a coincidence that is almost expected since John has warned Louise that Stephen is 'sure to have changed his mind and then we would be in a mess' (*SBC* 186). Finding her and John together in the bath, Stephen pushes Louise out into the street in her dressing gown. This in turn motivates Louise's appeal by telephone to Sarah because 'You're my sister ... There's no one else I dare ask' (*SBC* 190–91), an appeal probably the more acceptable as they have just spent the evening together.

This event supplies a satisfactorily emphatic climax to the plot. Stephen's emotions have exploded as foreseen, and the crumbling of the artificial situation that Louise has imposed upon other people shows, as she says, that she was wrong to expect other individuals to dance to her tune.

The main Sarah–Louise division then, between the character who watches and thinks, and the one who acts, is a strong basis for the plot, and on the sidelines the other characters in the novel are mainly drawn up in two camps – those who mete out news of the Louise affair to Sarah, and those offering a spectrum of lifestyles against which Sarah has to choose her own. The first group of characters are those helpful to a first-person narrator, who cannot be present at all the events in the observed plot, and who cannot see omnisciently into the thoughts of other people.

The other group of characters includes young married women like Gill and Stephanie, and also Sarah's unmarried cousin Daphne, the stereotypical unattractive young woman, probably doomed to spinsterhood, and so unlike the Bennett sisters that Louise says she is 'like a different species ... There's really no point in pretending that she's a human being like me, because she so obviously isn't'(*SBC* 164). Louise formulates a distinction between 'carnivores' like herself and other successful people, and inept failures like Daphne who are 'herbivores', and exist only to make the carnivores feel successful. Daphne also introduces an anxious concern about unfairness in human destiny, which recurs in several Drabble novels: 'I don't deserve to be as I am: she doesn't deserve to be as she is' (*SBC* 168).

Margaret Drabble was deprecating about *A Summer Bird-Cage*, commenting, 'I look at it and I think, Oh God, I might at least have tried',[5] but the novel shows that, with or without conscious organization, she produced an economical structure on two levels with a clear-cut plot progression that follows the classic Oedipus pattern of revealing the meaning of events in the light of revelations from the past.

Again, *The Garrick Year*, in spite of its title, does not in fact extend its action over a full year, though it covers a slightly longer period than *A Summer Bird-Cage*. Drabble focuses on the seven months during which Emma Evans has to accompany her actor husband to Hereford: he is taking part in a prestigious repertory season in a brand-new theatre there. The 'year', then, is a spring and summer season, including the preliminary rehearsal period, and the Evans family go there in February and leave in the early autumn. The choice of this defined period and temporary place seems to have the effect of isolating Emma and emphasizing her predicament, a logical next stage from Sarah's anxieties about marriage and identity.

Emma is a different kind of personality from Sarah, but has the same intelligence and reflectiveness, equipping her as another articulate first-person narrator: Drabble says, 'I am aware that my characters tend to be not only intelligent, but intelligent about themselves'.[6] Emma is already, before the excursion to Hereford, suffering from the strains of marriage and two children under the age of 2, but has apparently retained some remnants of her own social life, and also occasionally works in the glamour profession of modelling (she is very tall, slim and striking in appearance). In addition, she has just been offered a job as one of the first women newsreaders on television, at a time when the television channels and the public were still unwilling to accept that women could be taken seriously in such a role. In order to accompany her husband David to Hereford, therefore, she has to give up this exceptionally lucky opportunity.

If the novel had been set in London Emma's situation would not have been the same, even without a prestigious new job: she would have had to be shown in a well established social context, with her own friends and resources. The seven-month exile in Hereford then emphasizes that she has to exist for this period of time solely as a wife and mother. This is galling for Emma, who establishes herself as a strong-willed person of idiosyncratic tastes who likes to get her own way. In this case, David, her equally strong-willed husband, has won a long-drawn-out conflict.

The plot is at first uneventful; here Emma's search for something to fill the boredom of provincial isolation is eventually rewarded by an affair with the celebrated director of the theatre season, Wyndham Farrer. He is the most powerful man in her circle, and his attention flatters her, raising something of the same addictive terror and excitement that she had felt when she first met David. Nonetheless, Emma is unwilling for their affair to progress to a sexual level; she also describes herself as currently resisting David's sexual approaches, not merely because she resents his involving her in the Hereford trip but because she claims to be constantly tired, with breast-feeding the baby who wakes in the night, a kind of frigidity found also in Rosamund and the younger Jane Gray. Thus she and Wyndham go out for meals while David is at the theatre, and drive around the countryside, but after some inept planning that keeps going wrong, they remain chaste until just before the end of the season.

At this point, there is suddenly a lot of action. Emma discovers that David is having an affair with a young actress, and while she is trying to absorb this situation, Flora, their 2-year-old daughter falls in the river, so Emma jumps in to rescue her. Finally, as she lies in bed with the resulting bad cold, suffering

Wyndham's ill-timed advances, she thinks: 'I really might as well give in: there was after all everything on the side of submission, and nothing to be gained by resistance except a purely technical chastity' (*GY* 161). The long-delayed consummation is immediately followed by the further accident of Wyndham's crushing Emma against the side of the garage as he tries to reverse into the road. While she is convalescing, her friend Julian, a minor character, drowns himself.

This introduction of dramatic plot events is quite common towards the end of Drabble novels: the discovery of Louise in the bath with her lover by her outraged husband, the car crash in *The Waterfall* and the baby's illness in *The Millstone* could all be seen as similar productions of a startling crisis to brighten up the story. The conclusion of *The Garrick Year*, however, emphasizes the interest Drabble feels in unpredictable accidents. Emma has asserted: 'life is governed by accidents' (*GY* 29) but none of the almost disastrous accidents really affect the plot: their more significant effect is to remind the characters and the reader that devastation could strike at any point. This is something that Drabble wanted to incorporate into her work: 'I think we delude ourselves if we think we can control events by understanding them. These moments are bound to happen and I suppose as a writer I'm showing that you can't control things ... Events have to dominate characters from time to time'. But she added: 'I don't like events to dominate them too much. I like a degree of self-control and self-propulsion, but that may be a deep psychological flaw in me'.[7]

Emma proposes the idea, found also in *A Summer Bird-Cage*, that individuality, the identity, the self, is a superstructure built on what is universally human or even animal – the compound of instincts, physical structures and impulses that are below the level of conscious control. It is the subterranean uncontrolled part of her which had originally attracted her to David, in a mixture of sexual desire and craving for the physical reactions – not exactly sexual but linked to sexuality in fear and excitement – which he causes in her: 'I myself, the surface of me, felt calm and dead and white in that unnatural glare, and the part of me that was not me, but just any old thing, the inside of me, the rubbish, was blazing away, shuddering like some augur's sacrifice'. (*GY* 24)

At this early stage, the image of the augur's sacrifice (from Webster's *The White Devil,* one of the plays in the Hereford season) is associated with Emma's sacrifice of her own wishes, but it also relates to her almost involuntary sliding into the affair with Wyndham. Though Drabble later said she had lost interest in the issue of consciousness, the powerful, irresistible force of sexual passion continues to appear in her repertoire of unpredictable accidents, usually to dangerous effect.[8] Indeed, at the beginning of the affair with Wyndham, Emma perceives 'clearly what later became confused, that I was about to be chained, in a fashion so arbitrary that it frightened me, to a passion so accidental that it confirmed nothing but my own inadequacy and inability to grow' (*GY* 90).

At the end of the narrative, it is, however, conscious choice that wins out over accident and the uncontrolled unconscious self. To Wyndham, Emma says, 'I want now, I want now, I want now', but he replies, 'People who get married give up the here and now for the sake of the hereafter, didn't you know?' (*GY* 161). Taking this to heart, she puts an end to the affair with the chivalric Wyndham, which clearly has no future, in the interests of the more insistent demands of motherhood. As Drabble said later, 'Life isn't fair, life isn't easy, and not everybody can be happy ... But I agree with the feminists in that I don't like people to give in. I believe in continued effort. I think that my characters go in for continued effort'.[9]

The final few pages of the novel recount a last picnic in the Hereford countryside, an idyllic conclusion that recurs in several Drabble novels, but here, undermining the idyll, Emma (alone) sees a sick, immobilised sheep which has a venomous snake hidden in its fleece. The balance to this startlingly gothic vision is Emma's own common sense, banal defiance: 'One just has to keep on and to pretend, for the sake of the children, not to notice' (*GY* 172). Accident or fate can always drown one's child or crush one under a car, and some characters, like the actor Julian, may succumb to suicide, but experience and environment, and especially parenthood, enlist the main characters among those who struggle and keep on.

Emma at least believes that her marriage is going to last for a long time, and she quotes from Hume on marriage as 'naturally' being 'of considerable duration' because of the need to bring up the offspring (GY 171): her acceptance implies a submission to the forces of nature.

She does not, it seems, change much during this novel, and the narrative is again a heuristic and eventually consolidatory process for her: she makes sense of her present situation by looking into the past, at her consumptive, alcoholic mother and her tolerant, survivalist father. Drabble however questions whether her resolutions are really long-term: 'Emma says, yes, although I'm a mad modern woman, I will do this for a little bit. That's what she says, in effect ... I'll bet she went off wildly once those children were off at school',[10] and warns that not all aspects of her nature are admirable. Drabble says she started the novel as a third-person account, giving quite a critical view of this assertive, unsociable young woman, but found that the method was not working and began again in the first-person form which can easily mask less attractive traits.[11]

In the third successive first-person narrative that Drabble produced, *The Millstone*, chance is also prominent and interacts with the revelation of character. A major theme is whether a character can be modified by events, given the tendency to remain stubbornly the same. Emma Evans had not changed, supporting Drabble's view that 'I think we have a very small area of free choice ... We can choose not to be selfish or as self-indulgent or as hard-working as we are by nature. We can choose to go against our nature, but only very slightly.'[12] Drabble said that she had decided to write about the way that childbirth can change a character, and deliberately arranged the circumstances so that her heroine would be as isolated as possible from other influences – a situation even more isolated than Emma's.[13] The last exchange of the novel expresses the feelings of its chief character, Rosamund Stacey, about personality:

> 'It's my nature. There's nothing I can do about my nature, is there?'
> 'No,' said George, his hand upon the door. 'No, nothing.' (M 172)

Yet Rosamund does change to some extent, because of the accidents which the plot inflicts upon her. Firstly she becomes pregnant on her first and only sexual encounter of the novel; then, after coming to terms with life as a single parent, she finds that her baby daughter Octavia has a serious heart defect, requiring an operation with only a four to one chance of success. Although the baby survives, Rosamund presents herself at the end of the novel as one who has become capable of deeper emotions, and has even extended her knowledge of the lives of others, but her maternal love for her child has locked out any other kind of relationship. (Drabble says, however, that she envisages Rosamund as marrying later on. This devotion to the baby, exclusively, is temporary but necessary and natural.[14])

One of the related changes is the intense focus of Rosamund's attention on her responsibility for her baby, as she herself acknowledges that she has had to eschew the luxury of ethical debate and concern for the feelings of others; indeed, her own feelings and impulses are hardening against claims that would previously have raised an instant response in her:

> When I was young, I used to be so good-natured. I used to see the best in everyone, to excuse all faults, to put all malice and shortcoming down to environment: in short, to take all blame upon myself. But for the child, I might have gone on like that forever and, who knows, I might have been the better and nicer for it in the kindness of my innocence. I repeat; not being blind, I saw faults but I excused them. Now I felt less and less like finding excuses. I still cringed politely and smiled when doors slammed in my face, but I felt resentment in my heart. (M 80)

So she has to admit that, 'as I grow older, I find myself changing a little' and adds 'I ... contemplated my growing selfishness, and thought that this was probably maturity' (M 145). This self-ishness is dramatically illustrated in the episode where Rosamund is forbidden to see her baby daughter in the hospital after the operation (a topic very much being canvassed in the early sixties), and has to scream herself into hysterics before the administrators give way.

Selfishness is the negative side of Rosamund's change, and her understanding of complete and overwhelming love, love for her daughter, is the positive side, a love which overshadows her romantic, unrequited and adolescent love for the baby Octavia's father, the pleasant but elusive George. Both love and self-ishness are tested by the extreme crisis of the baby's dangerous illness: it is one function of this accidental plot event to emphasize the intensity and exclusivity of the maternal love that Rosamund feels, as the normal course of events would have allowed it to remain hidden. Similarly, the explicit effect of the first accident of the plot – her unmarried pregnancy, undergone without the support and advice of husband, parents or siblings – is to bring Rosamund face to face with the plight of the less privileged majority of the population, about which she has previously had very little knowledge: the other pregnant women and mothers are 'representatives of a population whose existence I had hardly noticed' (*M* 37). Her first visit to her new doctor in a poor district is 'a revelation: it was an initiation into a new way of life, a way that was thenceforth to be mine forever. An initiation into reality, if you like' (*M* 36).

In the maternity clinic, Rosamund looks at the rest of humanity and realizes in a Wordsworthian way 'that I felt a stranger and a foreigner there, and yet I was one of them, I was like that too, I was trapped in a human limit for the first time in my life, and I was going to have to learn how to live inside it' (*M* 58). It is interesting that Drabble does not make maternity one hundred per cent beneficial and promoter of the ultimate good – as with the boredom her mothers sometimes feel, she is depicting a realistic rather than an idealistic experience.

Rosamund, even more than Emma, looks to the past to try to assess how she has got to this situation. She blames her accidental but prolonged lack of sexual experience, her own unwillingness to become involved with other human beings. Highly self-aware, she realizes that her detachment has meant she was unprepared to take relationships seriously. Her thoughts about her pregnancy at first present it as a punishment, a supernatural message that she has been too indecisive about sex, too lacking in commitment: 'I got it thus, my punishment, because I had dallied and hesitated and trembled for too long' (*M* 18). She sees the influence of some kind of intentional moral force:

> At times I had a vague and complicated sense that this pregnancy had been sent to me in order to reveal to me a scheme of things totally different from the scheme which I inhabited, totally removed from academic enthusiasms, social consciousness, etiolated undefined emotional connections, and the exercise of free will. It was as though for too long I had been living in one way, on one plane, and the way I had ignored had been forced thus abruptly and violently to assert itself. Really, it was a question of free will; up to this point

in my life I had always had the illusion at least of choice, and now for the first time I seemed to become aware of the operation of forces not totally explicable, and not therefore necessarily blinder, smaller, less kind or more ignorant than myself. (*M* 67)

This lesson is reinforced when Rosamund holds a baby for an overwhelmed, large mother who also has a toddler and is already pregnant again – 'the word that was written on her was endurance' (*M* 70). When Rosamund sees her again outside the clinic, she is able to enter into the experience of this woman and those like her, because she has felt the weight of the baby. 'There was a solemnity about her imperceptible progress that impressed me deeply', she reflects, as the woman moves slowly along the street, like Wordsworth's leech gatherer,[15] 'like a warning, like a portent, like a figure from another world' (*M* 71). The warning is, however, of loss of independence, the need to ask for help from strangers, and yet she shows that this can be endured, and if by her, then surely by Rosamund too.

Drabble plays with the idea of chance and coincidence in Rosamund's plight, first and most obviously because a woman is unlikely to become pregnant from her first and only sexual experience. Then, Rosamund's attempt to bring on an abortion by the traditional method of drinking a lot of gin in a hot bath is foiled jointly by the coincidence of friends arriving at her flat just as she is about to embark on this, and by her own ingrained good manners in offering them the gin to drink, thus leaving herself not enough for any chance of success with the abortion. Here, as with her attempt to contact a professional abortionist, which she abandons after only one attempt when the phone number is engaged, it can be argued that it is not coincidence or fate but Rosamund's own personality which is responsible – she could after all easily have turned her friends away with some excuse and proceeded with the gin and hot bath if she had been determined to do so, or even have bought more gin the next day, or kept trying to phone the abortionist until she got an answer.

Yet she goes on to reject the concept of punishment, or even of malignant or careless deities injuring individuals at random, returning to the idea that there is some kind of meaning in her experiences, and that she will find the link. In this novel, the meaning as suggested above seems to emerge as Rosamund's development from a young woman with theoretical views about social justice and personal relationships to one who is forced to experience them intimately – 'I had always felt for others in theory and pitied the blows of fate and circumstance under which they suffered; but now, myself no longer free, myself suffering, I may say that I felt it in my heart' (M 68).

As well as the main two accidents, there are other smaller coincidences that facilitate the plot, such as the surgeon who treats Octavia being a close friend of Rosamund's parents, and thus not only sympathetic to her but able to inform her parents about her baby and its plight. Thinking of such ironies, Rosamund suggests that her interest 'had been a premonition of a different, non-rational order of things' and becomes 'convinced that my state must have some meaning, that it must, however haphazard and unexpected and unasked, be connected to some sequence, to some significant development of my life' (M 66–7). Although her later understanding of the nature of life for the majority of mothers is an important result, it does not quite amount to 'some link ... that would make sense of disconnections' (M 67).

All these three novels have first-person narrators who take the reader into their confidence in their own way. All of them are sincere, as far as they understand themselves and their situations, but not all of them do understand their situations very well. Sarah is very straightforward in her narrative, and the plot depends on the gradual revelation of what she does not know, but Emma is indifferent and perhaps unaware of the effect she has on other people. Rosamund's delicacy in not pressing on George any relationship that he has not seemed to seek himself results for him in the loss of a daughter, or at least the loss of the opportunity to decide whether he wants to take up his paternal role or not. Drabble says that Rosamund 'is guilty of putting George in a very false situation. She behaves much worse than he does. He is vague only in that she can't see him clearly'.[16] Drabble wanted to escape from the limitation of the first-person point of view, and had found she was unable to do it in *The Garrick Year*; it was in her next two novels that she managed, though only partially, to cross this barrier.

28

4

An Event Seen from an Angle

Although Margaret Drabble began to use the third-person narrator in her next two novels, these can be seen as transitional in that the point of view is still limited mainly or totally to that of the female protagonist. *Jerusalem the Golden* is the first of Drabble's novels not to be written in the first-person, but the narrative keeps so closely to the point of view of Clara Maugham, its main character, that the effect is almost that of another first-person text. Drabble has spoken of the failings of the other early heroines, such as Emma Evans's wildness and Rosamund's 'dryness of the spirit',[1] but she has made much harsher comments about Clara ('I don't *like* her very much. I think she's my most unsympathetic heroine, in many ways – she's an elitist at heart'[2]) even though she might seem at first reading merely to be a more provincial version of the observant Sarah Bennett. But Clara is a little more limited, selfish and unimaginative than her predecessors, and her initiation into wider experiences does not necessarily make her a nicer person.

Some years later, in 1974, Drabble wrote a biography of Arnold Bennett, whose work she had always admired: she wrote it 'in a partisan spirit, as an act of appreciation' (AB vii) and acknowledges 'my own debt to Bennett in *Jerusalem the Golden*' (AB 47–8), which she feels was strongly influenced by the same kind of attitudes. Clara was much like the typical Bennett character, especially Hilda Lessways, being intent on escape and ready for adventure and new experiences – Drabble adds 'my novel is almost as much an appreciation of Bennett as this book is meant to be' (AB 48).

The focalization on Clara, representing the world as seen by her, expressing her anxieties and misgivings, tends to engage the reader's sympathy for her. One or two comments are directed at Clara within the narrative, as mentioned below, but these are unobtrusive and easily overlooked. Chance, also seen as luck, is important in this novel. Clara refers to her luck in escaping her background: her family is a repressive lower-class unit, dominated by a mother who is the first of the monster-mothers who also loom over the childhoods of Kate Armstrong and Liz Headland. Unlike the chilly, frigid, pretentious mothers of Jane Gray, Simon Camish or Frances Wingate, Mrs Maugham is embittered, domineering and confrontational.

In the retrospective sections of the narrative, we see the schoolgirl Clara fleeing a home where she is always in the wrong, and throwing herself enthusiastically into the freedom of the stark, traditional grammar school in the large industrial city of Northam where she was born. Northam, 'that figurative northern city' (RW 47) reappears frequently in the novels, a bleak version of Drabble's own home city of Sheffield, and Clara hates it bitterly, seeing it as an extension of her mother and her home. She is delighted to leave it for London University, and is overcome with depression at having to return home for the vacations. Her ideas of the wider world are mainly culled from books and magazines, and at the beginning of the novel she is still longing for a glimpse of the sophistication which her student life in London has not yet shown her.

The second stage of her 'luck' lies in her gaining the entrée into a network of relationships among interesting and attractive people, more successful and distinguished than any she has known before. At a poetry reading, she first meets the Denhams – Sebastian Denham is a middle-aged, established poet, and his daughter Clelia, also present at the reading, is to become Clara's close friend. Friendship is always important in Drabble's novels, and seems to survive where love affairs fade and disappear. From this encounter springs all the remaining action of the novel, and there is narrative emphasis on how accidental and precarious this encounter was: 'Sometimes she wondered what would have happened if she had missed them, and whether a conjunction so fateful and fruitful could have been, by some accidental obtuseness on her part, avoided' (JG 9); apart from the chance nature of the meeting, she might well have failed to notice Clelia's unique personality, as indeed she had overlooked her for the first few minutes:

30

she could not forget that she had not recognized it at once, that it had required on her part some keenness of perception, some chancy courage to see it; and she breathed perpetually an air of terror, a cold air of chance, an air in which she might for the whole of her life have missed it, marginally perhaps, but missed it and forever. (*JG* 25)

On the other hand, in spite of her determination to make something of herself, Clara is one of the most obsessed of all the Drabble characters with heredity and upbringing: Kate Armstrong and Liz Headleand are older and have many other preoccupations, but Clara is still locked in the relationship with her mother and fears the emotional blackmail that may force her to return to live and work in Northam. The meeting with the Denhams opens the novel, beginning the main sequence of events in the plot, but all the information about Clara's childhood, her harsh mother and Northam Grammar School is introduced after this, in the exceptionally long flashback in the second, third and fourth chapters.

In the set-piece description of Clara's school trip to Paris at 17, she goes alone to Montmartre at night, picks up an Italian young man and goes to the cinema with him. At one level, it teaches Clara, though only as an afterthought, that the rules of schools, and of provincial life, are not unbreakable. It is possible to interpret this episode as introducing hints of an existential wilfulness into her character: she grasps the suggestion that she can choose, she can make her own choices without being limited by outside pressures. This appears in some of her decisions, but not all, and she is not able to exercise this freedom of choice when it comes to cutting herself off from her mother. She struggles to remain at a distance from her home, but without the ruthless decisiveness that her friends urge upon her:

she did not see that she could leave Northam for ever. She felt herself restrained from such freedom. And she sought, faintly, for compromise, for some way of life that would enable her to see her mother as often as a sense of duty obliged. She never allowed herself to suspect that duty might oblige her to return entirely, but this idea lay in the back of her head, as of some final, exhausting, bleeding martyrdom. (*JG* 82–3)

Outside the range of Northam, Clara is able to live her own life; she has made many trips abroad in the vacations, on the pretext of her degree studies in French, and has had many boyfriends in

London. Because she has to fight against the early pressures of her upbringing on her character, she shapes her life as best she can by will-power. On the negative side, this makes her say 'I am too full of will to love', which, in a rare authoritative intervention, the narrator confirms: 'love, desperately, eluded her; she had not been taught to love, she had lacked those expensive, private lessons' (JG 165).

On a more positive level, she is inspired to imagine examples of experiences which will be quite unlike her home. Hence the rather artificial constructed nature of her attitude to life: not being spontaneous, she pictures a life based on her reading and filmgoing, and tries to seek it out or to make it happen. To her surprise, when she meets the Denhams, this life takes on reality:

> she had begun to think that she had created herself, through her own imagination, the whole genre. She had wanted such people to exist, so dressed, so independent, so involved; she had needed them, so she had presupposed them. And here, as she slowly realized, was a woman who was the thing that she had presupposed. She stood, and watched the felicity of her own invention, and experienced the satisfaction of her recognition. (JG 20)

Similarly, her ambition to become involved in an interesting and complex relationship is fulfilled when she begins an affair with the extremely attractive Gabriel Denham, one of Clelia's brothers, who is unhappily married. Her reaction is again of surprise and satisfaction: 'She had presupposed such a man as Gabriel, such a dark and surreptitious lunch, such an episode upon an unfamiliar floor, and it had happened to her. She felt triumphant' (JG 159). Like Frances Wingate, she seems to share her (implied) author's powers of invention and creation, making her own plot happen. The fulfilment of her fantasies almost alarms her because of the unexpected luck that she sees in it; the laws of chance seem to be overcoming heredity and background in a way she never expected.

More clearly documented are the influences of Clara's harsh, unloved childhood. The early chapters have established her tense struggles to evade the iron hand of this upbringing, and frequent reminders of how it has nonetheless shaped her behaviour recur throughout the novel – for instance, she is amazed to find herself able to respond to Clelia's welcoming embrace, because 'she had not been reared upon embraces' (JG 116).

The explanation of one's nature as shaped by heredity and upbringing, attempted so far vestigially by Emma, and more extensively by Rosamund, becomes more dominant from this novel onward. The anxieties of Clara are more acute and simple than those of later characters, in that she regards both the tensions and hesitations of her own character and the pressures exerted on her as embodied in the person of her mother.

In a clandestine excursion to Paris with Gabriel, which structurally balances the first school trip to Paris in the narrative, she feels she has at last achieved the state of existential freedom so long eluding her. In a long sequence, she moves from one encounter to another with Gabriel's colleagues and chance-met acquaintances, eased by the plentiful glasses of wine in cafés and restaurants. Drabble's style here shifts to a simple accumulative series of descriptive statements linked with 'And ... so ... then ... and', as experiences wash over Clara with dream-like ease. She feels strangely clear and light, and, freed from her normal anxieties and tensions, decides arbitrarily to leave Gabriel sleeping and travel back home alone.

> ... she felt free, the light weight of her limbs, the clear grey spaces in her head, the ebbing of her need, these were merely symptoms of her freedom, and she was in some open early region where despair and hope seemed, as words, quite interchangeable, where she seemed to sit, quite calmly, beside her own fate ... The complete equality of all actions assailed her, solaced her; there was really no difference, it was all the same, Orly, Le Bourget, lipstick, no lipstick, sleep, no sleep, none of it seemed to matter. (JG 188)

This fallacious impression is necessary to give her the sense of being able to choose, but, as suggested by the word 'fate', it is merely a temporary indifference. Clara has excused her absence to her director of studies by claiming that she has to visit her mother who is ill: by a fine dramatic coincidence, she returns to her London lodgings to find a telegram saying that her mother is indeed seriously ill. This is the end of Clara's nonchalant freedom:

> When Clara opened the telegram and saw the news about her mother, she trembled as though she had been struck from the heavens. She stood there, staring at the fatal yellow paper, and her first thought was, I have killed my mother. By willing her death, I have killed her. By taking her name in vain, I have killed her. She

thought, let them tell me no more that we are free, we cannot draw a breath without guilt, for my freedom she dies. And she felt closing in upon her, relentlessly, the hard and narrow clutch of retribution, those iron fingers which she had tried, so wilfully, so desperately to elude; a whole system was after her, and she the final victim, the last sacrifice, the shuddering product merely of her past. (*JG* 191)

It would clearly take more than a wine-sprinkled afternoon and evening in Paris to eradicate the responses that make up much of Clara's nature.

Later, looking at her mother's relics in the empty house, Clara finds old photographs showing her mother as young, hopeful and tender, and, even more unsettling, exercise books in which her mother had once written stories and poems. This is a shock, because it reinforces the powers of both heredity and luck, diminishing the impression of free will that has been so fleeting. The episode is one that is repeated in later novels – the physical searching through drawers and cupboards, down through the layers of old clothes and papers, produces evidence from an earlier era; the past comes to light. Although no more is said about it in the narrative, Clara's mother had evidently once been talented and ambitious, before she became the grim figure of misery that Clara has always known: 'It was possible, then, to go disastrously astray; tragedy was possible, survival was no certainty, there was no reason why anyone should escape' (*JG* 196).

Yet Drabble leaves the final sequence of the novel open. Clara has decided, she says, to break off her relationship with Gabriel, but she looks forward to his driving her back to London, down the motorway, on a journey that, like other Drabble heroines, she will enjoy for its sense of movement and speed and openness. As long as one is travelling, one is uncommitted and unlimited, and Clara hopes for an endless branching series of opportunities, as yet undetermined. She has decided to rely on chance and will-power.

The novel, then, mainly offers Clara's own interpretation of events, and to that extent is very close to the preceding first-person narratives; but at times the narrator adds a comment which offers a supplementary and sometimes hostile point of view. It is the narrator who underlines Clara's inability to love Gabriel as she claims to, though implying that it is not Clara's fault that she 'lacked those expensive private lessons'. More sharply, Clara's selfishness in avoiding hospitality is criticized, with acknowledgement of her self-knowledge alongside criticism of her lack of knowledge of the feelings of others:

> And she was, too, incurably mean and lazy; she would rather any day be guest than hostess, she would rather reach out her hand for a drink than wash out a glass and lift up a bottle to pour one. She never entertained, and could not see that she ever would ... It never crossed her mind that others might feel a similar reluctance; she expected to be on the receiving end. (*JG* 132)

It is often difficult when a narrator is focalizing on a character's reactions to distinguish the character's own thoughts from the narrator's judgements, but although Clara is said to accuse herself of avarice, idleness and ineptitude, the final sentence about what 'never crossed her mind' is unmistakably a comment by the narrator on her blindness.

Gabriel Denham is the other character who is given brief sections of focalization: when Clara is unsympathetic to the story of an errant wife returning for her child, 'he could see that the thought of a child meant nothing to her, as indeed how should it'. Gabriel compares her with his sister Clelia who has accepted the motherless baby with tenderness, and the narrator adds that 'he thought that he saw in Clara a more voracious simplicity' (*JG* 150): the 'he thought' implies a doubt of his accuracy here. Similarly his impressions of Clara as warm and enthusiastic are undermined by the phrasing of 'Clara seemed to him, in his ignorance, to be everything that Phillipa was not' (*JG* 140).

In spite of the open ending, then, it is an indictment of Clara that she has not been able to reconcile herself with her mother at any point. She does not bring any flowers to her mother in hospital at the end:

> she had been afraid, afraid of rejection ... She had been afraid of the gesture; she had learned nothing, she could not give, and yet she knew that without gestures there was no hope that love might fill the empty frames, the extended arms, the social kisses, the proffered flowers. She had brought nothing, and her meanness dismayed her. She had not wished to be mean. (*JG* 198)

This is mainly Mrs Maugham's fault for repressing all tenderness, but even so, Clara, who has changed so much in other ways, is not able to change herself here: 'with relief she saw that there would be nothing, that she would not be called upon to give, that she could merely answer meanness with meanness' (*JG* 200). This tight grip of upbringing on her character in the end undermines the apparent hopefulness of her future.

Margaret Drabble was not totally satisfied with this first excursion into the third-person point of view, which had departed very little from the first-person form of the earlier novels, and tried to vary the form thereafter. *The Waterfall* is one of the most experimental narratives Drabble has written so far, in spite of her claims to have been still naïve at this stage. She was to use multiple points of view frequently in her later work, but in *The Waterfall* there is a systematically unsettling alternation between first-person and third-person narrative, and the unreliability of these narratives is proclaimed at intervals by the more probing first-person narrator, who criticizes not only the third-person sections but also her own first-person version of events.

The Waterfall concentrates, like its predecessors, on the experience of a single female character, and tells of the love affair of Jane Gray with James Otford, the husband of her cousin Lucy. Jane, separated from her own husband, is the central character of the plot and is also the narrator, sometimes telling about her experiences in the third person, referring to herself as 'she' and 'Jane', and sometimes as a first-person narrator using 'I'.

From the very first sentence, the novel is deceptive, starting as it does without quotation marks 'If I were drowning I couldn't lift a hand to save myself ...' (*W* 7), so that the reader, perhaps knowing Drabble's preference for the form, thinks 'Ah, a first-person narrative' – but the second sentence continues 'This is what she said to him one night' and immediately the reader has to readjust to a third-person narrative. This small trick is indicative of the shifts of perspective that recur throughout the novel. The third-person sections of the text focus particularly on Jane Gray's feelings and reactions, a narrowness of focus enhanced by her claims to be mentally frail – ' "I'm mad," she said, "I'm wicked, and I'm mad" ' (*W* 73) – and not only unfitted for close personal relationships but unable to face ordinary everyday contact with other people, such as meeting other mothers at a nursery group, responding to remarks from familiar shopkeepers, or even passing people in the street. The world of the third-person narrative shrinks to a small circle enclosing Jane, her two children, her lover James. Other people, like the nursery group mothers, appear briefly only to show her sense of alienation or tactics of avoidance.

The first-person sections have a wider remit, and not only include all the retrospective expositionary material about Jane's childhood, hostility to her parents, relationship with her cousin Lucy, marriage to Malcolm and the failure of that marriage, but also criticize and undermine the third-person narrative sections:

> It won't, of course, do: as an account, I mean, of what took place. I tried, I tried for so long to reconcile, to find a style that would express it, to find a system that would excuse me, to construct a new meaning, having kicked the old one out, but I couldn't do it, so here I am, resorting to that old broken medium ... (W 46)

What appears here is a dual narrative approach, which deliberately undermines itself. First-person Jane narrates third-person Jane, then comments on her own efforts, so, as in *A Summer Bird-Cage*, there is a basic story, a fabula, which Drabble has worked on and transformed by adding two different layers of meaning. The basic events are first dressed in the guise of a traditional love story, given by the third-person narrator, which in itself is a choice of presentation. The first-person narrator then adds to this the psychological and social dimensions which do not so much anchor the love story in reality as undermine it by questioning, not just Jane's truthfulness, but the possibility of ever understanding the conditions of any human situation: 'the ways of regarding an event, so different, don't add up to a whole; they are mutually exclusive' (W 46). It is in the first-person sections that Jane explores the influences of the past, questioning her dependence on her cousin Lucy, who dominates and fascinates her rather as Louise had dominated Sarah. Jane's parents are described with hostility as having blighted her life with their insensitive hypocritical upbringing of their family.

The main substance of the novel deals with the nature and validity of Jane's and James's affair, entwined as it is with the nature of Jane's own character. Margaret Drabble emphasizes that she intended to assert the importance of romantic love:

I can see why feminists don't like it – because it's about a passionate heterosexual love affair which disturbs everything. It disturbs all one's preconceptions about what's important in life. I think passionate heterosexual love affairs are extremely important and that whole book is devoted to one. People who don't like that kind of stuff aren't going to like the book. They're going to disbelieve the premise that this emotion is real. So they find the heroine unattractive and her submission to her fate lamentable and the texture of the book unpleasant. I don't care about that. I wasn't writing it for them.[3]

The third-person sections are, we understand, written by first-person Jane, and are, therefore and confusingly, all part of her narrative: her views of James are consistent in both parts. Margaret Drabble explains the results of this:

when he does something which doesn't fit in with her view of him, then she can hardly bring herself to say he did it ... she doesn't bother to tell you all the other things he did and was, which would have made him a full person. That's a characteristic of most romantic fiction, that characters don't do the things that would undo the romantic fiction ... it seems to me that in a first-person novel you can have only one full person, and that's the first person.[4]

Third-person Jane lives in a world where everything outside her immediate desires and anxieties fades away into distorted shadows: either she refuses to think about external problems, like her husband Malcolm who is blotted from her mind, or else she sees small obstacles, such as the turnstile at the zoo, as insuperable barriers that will involve her in catastrophic conflict and failure. She wants her love for James to maintain its purity and intensity untainted by everyday life. This mythic tone is set in the first pages when Jane awaits the birth of her second baby, in an upstairs bedroom alone in her house, with snow falling outside, like a heroine of romance in an ivory tower.

Margaret Drabble has commented that she felt uncomfortable having written this initial episode:

I'd been wanting to write the first section of the book for a long time, and I wrote it and I was intending to turn it into a novel. When I'd written it, I couldn't go on, because it seemed to me that I'd set up this very forceful image of romantic, almost thirteenth-century love. Having had the experience or describing the experience, one had to say what is this about? I thought the only way to do it was to make Jane say it.[5]

As in several early Drabble novels, crisis strikes near the end of the plot. James, Jane and her children are driving north for a clandestine holiday in Norway when a road accident leaves James near death, and Jane is thus stranded with him in an anonymous midland town. She remarks that the narrative could have ended artistically with James's death at this point: 'There isn't any conclusion. A death would have been the answer, but nobody died. Perhaps I should have killed James in the car, and that would have made a neat, a possible ending. A feminine ending?' (W 230–31). Another potential heroic closure is evoked, then evaded, in that Lucy necessarily finds out about their love affair when she learns about the accident. After a first outburst of rage, however, Lucy does not demand any crucial action. Neither Lucy nor Jane renounces James, and in spite of the catastrophic nature of the car crash, the concluding pages tell us that life proceeds much as before, indeed perhaps even more securely, as she now does not have to fear Lucy's finding out. This rejection of closure is deliberate: the first-person narrator tells us 'It's odd that there should be no ending' (W 232).

The first-person narrator has accused herself of twisting the events, mainly by selective omission, in order to present herself in the best possible light, and later reiterates 'Lies, lies, it's all lies. A pack of lies. I've even told lies of fact, which I had meant not to do. Oh, I meant to deceive, I meant to draw analogies, but I've done worse than that. I've misrepresented' (W 84). The most thorough and systematic critique of both narratives occurs towards the end. The crucial effect of the final events is the impact not on the injured James or on the James–Jane–Lucy triangle of relationships, but on the character of Jane herself, who not only retains her relationship with James, but reorganizes her crumbling house, her chaotic occupations and her relationships with other people into an approximation to normality. Because of the idea, repeated in other novels, that people do not change very much, events should in fact have a limited impact upon them, and Jane has believed that 'people could not change, that they were predetermined, unalterable, helpless in the hands of destiny... I have to rethink it all now, in terms of what I know myself to be' (W 227).

Drabble thus reconciles 'people could not change' with the changes to Jane by letting her suggest 'I had been perfectly all right all the time' (W 237):

> At the beginning of this book I deliberately exaggerated my helplessness, my dislocation, as a plea for clemency. So that I should not be judged. Poor helpless Jane, abandoned, afraid, timid, frigid, bereft. What right had anyone to point an accusing finger? Poor Jane, lying in that bed with her new-born child, alone. Poor Jane, child of such monstrous parents. How could she not be mad? ... There's nothing wrong with my parents, anyway. Quite often I like them. (W 226)

She has been using her apparent agoraphobia and other nervous habits as a strategy to gain what she wanted – love, a safe uninterrupted domestic life. It seems that this strategy was wielded unconsciously, but nonetheless at the end of the novel, with Jane's goals achieved, her neuroticism fades. The reader is asked to reconsider the activities of the character and see them as temporary and superficial, reconcilable with a basically competent, strong personality.

Yet Jane also suggests, in a mixture of Freudian determinism and mysticism, that her fate, her destiny, had been sought by herself. If she had not wanted a powerful love affair, then she would not have found one. This suggests that opportunities are attracted to those who want them, and that, as Liz says in a later book (RW 59–60), if you want something enough you will get it, but also that the inner core of the self rejects and accepts experiences until it gets what is right for itself, as Jane rejected Malcolm and accepted James.

By moving between the two levels of narrative, Drabble reminds the reader that events can be interpreted differently according to context, and that the narrative form affects the presentation of character; different things are selected, different emphases emerge. The sense of self derives from the stories that the individual tells about him- or herself, and Jane is divided between two master narratives, seeking to explain both halves of herself – the simple, powerful seeker for love, and the neurotic, observant product of her family and education. She claims that the former essential part of her is what James loved – 'When James looked at me he saw me, myself... It was my true self he saw' (W 51–2), and, unlike Emma Evans, Jane identifies the deeper part of herself with her essential self: 'for the bodily level was in many ways more profound, more human, more myself' (*W* 104).

The explanatory narrative also queries its own determinism – are the causes dredged up from the past really so influential, so sufficient? 'What after all was I complaining about?' asks Jane, 'An unhappy childhood, an unsatisfactory marriage, my own laziness' (*W* 227). Determinism is re-harnessed as a way of reinforcing the present: 'Had I been destined for collapse, I would have collapsed. But I was not' (*W* 228). A pattern is established here: when characters look into the past or into some other system of life to find an explanation or justification, the sources are ambiguous, or they recede into the past or depend on other, more remote causes in their turn. The sense of cause and effect is anxiously sought, but their validity is constantly undermined.

5

What Was the Point of Knowing What Was Right (If One Didn't Then Do It)?

The Needle's Eye is seen as marking a watershed in Margaret Drabble's writing; it focuses the action mainly through the eyes of a male character, Simon Camish, but also large parts of the narrative are focalized upon Simon's new friend, Rose Vassiliou, and more occasionally on various minor characters, glimpsed as leading their own full lives which occasionally intersect with those of the protagonists. The attachment to the single female protagonist is broken, and Drabble had achieved her ambition to write in the omniscient third-person narrator, moving flexibly among the minds of different characters. This is something like the method that appears in her later work, but she refers back to *The Needle's Eye* from within one of these later discursive novels, self-referentially, as being 'the old-fashioned, Freudian, psychological novel'(*GI* 461) in contrast to the freer, looser structure of her later work.

Also, perhaps as a natural progression, in *The Needle's Eye* Drabble gives some sense of a wider social perspective, where British society is shown in a more comparative and analytic way, pursuing the contrast between ways of life that Rosamund had begun to perceive in *The Millstone*. This contrast is represented initially by Simon's awareness of his own climb from grim poverty to his affluent lifestyle as a barrister. Then, reversing this, there is the depiction of Rose's deliberate rejection of her own wealthy upbringing to settle in a decaying terraced house in a deprived, unfashionable area of north London.

Again the structure of the novel is dualistic. As Sarah observed Louise's drama, and as Jane Gray split herself into the observed and the observer, here Simon observes the drama of Rose's life. The two meet at a dinner party, then the histories of both are told, mainly in the silent reminiscences of one or the other, but also, in Rose's case, in her own embedded narrative to Simon. An unwilling heiress, Rose had earlier achieved some notoriety in the media because she married Christopher Vassiliou in spite of her father's strenuous efforts to stop her. Rose then gained further notoriety by giving away her inheritance: as a child, neglected by her parents, she was influenced by a religious fundamentalist nursemaid, Noreen, and has grown up to hate wealth. Even though her father tried to disinherit her after her defiant marriage, Rose still has various sums coming to her from trust funds, and she gave one such fund to a small African country to build a school (which within two years was burnt down in civil war), a gesture which gave her another bout of publicity and established her as an unwilling speaker on the third world and poverty. When Simon first meets her, she is the mother of three small children, and is divorced from Christopher, who had bitterly resented her refusal to accept any part of her inheritance and her determination to continue living in such a run-down area of London. Christopher has just made a move to claim custody of their children. The main situation, which depicts Christopher's increasing threat to Rose's unobtrusive contentment and involves Simon's occasional efforts to help, depends on this custody claim.

It is important however to realize that the conflict of the novel is, at a deeper level, not between Rose and Christopher for their children, but an ideological one, between the prosperous materialist way of life to which Simon and his friends belong and the deliberately unambitious level at which Rose lives, and to which she has an almost mystical commitment. She is not fanatical about renouncing materialism – she has a television, she buys the children sweets and toys – but she does not compete. She sends her children to the local state primary school, and she never buys clothes. Beside the well furnished, well decorated house of her friends' dinner party, her small terraced house is a pointed contrast. 'How rich they all were',

Simon had thought, struggling to relate it to 'this society that complained so often in its newspapers of its ailing economy' (*NE* 14). Rose later explains that her limited life, considered mad by others, is a source of joy to her. She is not, like Jane Gray, deliberately letting her surroundings decay from sheer passivity and fear of failure: quite the contrary, Rose's longest explication of her attitudes and values insists on the actual pleasure of living as she does:

> I like it here precisely because it is dull, and because I can – oh, I don't know, clean my own shoes and worry about the electricity bill and look after my own children and collect them from school and take an interest in the Cheap Offers in the shops. Oh, I know, people think it's not real, they think it's nonsense for me to sit here like I do, they think I'm playing. They tell me that everyone else round here is miserable and all the rest of it. But they don't know, because they've never tried it. I do know. I respond to such ordinary signals in the world. Cut prices and sunshine and babies in prams and talking in the shops. (*NE* 111)

Much of the criticism of society is played out at the level of personal morality, with only occasional hints of social pressures, and this is emphasized by the drama of Rose's making such public and exemplary moral decisions about her life. Simon's life parallels some aspects of Rose's career, in that he, like Christopher Vassiliou, has married a rich man's daughter. Julie, a woman of little imagination, is very far from rejecting her paternal wealth, and consoles herself for her empty, superficial life by shopping and competing with her friends.

Rose thus attracts Simon by her absolute reversal of Julie's personality: Rose and Simon are in fact very much alike, and just as the attraction of opposites has drawn them to Christopher and Julie, a sympathy of tastes and attitudes brings them to each other. Their very low-key relationship however does not develop during the course of the novel beyond Simon's hypothetical 'If I had been free, I would have asked you to marry me' and Rose's acknowledgement: 'What a nice time we would have had. I too have thought of it, you know' (*NE* 321).

The novel deals with issues of duty and right and wrong, extended from the individual to society, but approaches them fairly tentatively and obliquely, in that Rose's position is so strongly criticized by almost all the other characters that the reader is not sure how far to admire her extreme stand. Drabble has admitted that Rose could be seen as 'a victim', the 'stereotype of the forgiving and docile woman',[1] but she herself disagrees:

> I admire Rose immensely. I don't see any reason why everyone should go out for material success and career success. I think Rose's decisions are perfectly valid, and I admire her way of life. She's not a loser at all – she's extremely resilient and psychologically success for her is avoiding what her history had destined her to be, which was to be a rich woman ...[2]

Simon's related but different position is that he endures the way of life he has come to hate by doing the work that he feels is worth doing. It is a meagre justification for his life, but at least it is a measurable justification, and his adherence to it, his 'resolution', is what holds his life together, and he is able to say to Rose 'I have been admirable in that I have fulfilled my obligations', though he has to add 'I've spent most of my time, I think, doing what on balance it seemed that I ought to do, not what I might have wanted to do, and now there isn't much that I do want to do' (*NE* 113). This too seems a process of arguable value.

And surprisingly Christopher is also given a moral point of view. Simon wants to believe that Christopher is a fortune hunter who has only married Rose for her potential inheritance, and has left her because she has rejected her wealth. But on meeting him Simon realizes that Christopher is a more complex figure than that; he is locked in a moral conflict with Rose, passionately believing that they belong together as a family and that she ought to accept those things that make their family life better. Ironically, he has become reconciled with Rose's father and now is a highly successful businessman. He believes Rose ought to have made the best of their relationship, and tells Simon 'She had no right to divorce me. And she knows it. And if she's happy now, as you say she is, she has no right to be. That's why I'm going to go on making trouble for her. Because she has no right to be happy. And I won't let her be so. You can't make happiness out of destroying the lives of other people' (*NE* 255).

Rose can be equally inflexible: she 'thought about the camel and the needle's eye. What was the point of knowing what was right, if one didn't then do it?' (*NE* 274). All in fact act according to character: Simon, against his own emotional interest in Rose, advises Christopher to return to live with her. In the end, this is what Christopher does, and he seeks to dominate his family from a more advantageous position. Nonetheless, Rose persists in remaining in the run-down house in the run-down area. Circumstances conspire to reduce their conflict, by causing the area to become rather more fashionable, so that Christopher gains some amelioration of a situation he dislikes, and also Rose, in spite of a deteriorating temper and loss of tranquillity, looks forward to some independence by going out to work. Simon in his turn benefits from the inclusion of Rose and her husband in his own social circle, and the gradual maturing and softening of Julie's character. Margaret Drabble has here handed out rewards and disappointments with a judicious hand, justifying her label of 'old fashioned Freudian psychological novel'.

In the background of the plot of conflict and character lie the forces of environment, heredity and coincidence. Like the characters in the previous three novels, Simon and Rose attribute their present attitudes and traits of personality to their upbringing. Rose re-enacts the recurrent symbolic scene of Drabble protagonists, first seen in Clara, when towards the end of the novel she goes to seek, in the cupboards and drawers of her substitute parent, Noreen, for some clue to explain the strong early influences upon her. Unlike Clara, Frances, Kate and Liz, Rose does not retrieve any explanatory object from the past: no book, diary or newspaper cuttings reward her search. She does however unearth a memory of testing out Noreen's assurances about the sharpness of razor blades: as a child she had found that a sharp razor does indeed cut flesh almost without effort, and so, written in blood, she had accepted all Noreen's other harsh, unrelenting teachings about punishment, exclusion and damnation. It is possible, then, to see Rose's quiet, undemanding life as a place of safety. By becoming poor, by making no claims, she has tried to protect herself from the plagues that are bound to fall upon the vain and the rich.

Simon too has been brought up by a strong female figure in the person of his ambitious but poverty-stricken mother who devoted herself to caring for a disabled husband and elderly father-in-law, investing all her ambitions in her son. Simon has writhed with embarrassment at his mother's excessive refinement and efforts to conceal their penury, as he worked his way up through grammar school, Oxford and city chambers. Now he sympathizes with her, but it is too late: they have diverged too far, she into a final achievement of South Coast gentility, and Simon into a revulsion against the wasteful consumer society he has climbed into.

Hence Simon has come to believe in 'hereditary woe', that 'people endure not one lifetime but many, many layers and layers of evolved suffering handed down, worse than anything Freud had ever proposed in the way of predestination' (NE 30), but he suspects that for Rose the shaping forces may go back to an earlier stage than Noreen's influence. As he has dinner with her and her parents, he thinks: 'People do not grow out of nothing, they do not spring from the earth. Somewhere in this house, in these two disagreeable ageing people, in this dingy dining room, lay the grounds for her fantastic notions' (NE 338). The theme of further causes underlying causes is a recurrent one, but here it is left ambiguous, and all the reader knows is the comparative neglect that has left Rose's childhood vulnerable to Noreen's indoctrination.

The word 'predestination' is recurrent in Drabble's novels, yet it is not entirely accurate for the fate of her characters, whose natures are an unpredictable mixture of heredity, education and accidental events. The mixed nature of heredity is not only twisted in Simon and Rose because they react against their dominant parents, but it is not clear how much contribution is made by their less assertive parents – Simon's paralysed, mentally ruined father and Rose's withdrawn, hypochondriac mother. The point is made more clearly about the conflict of influences on the Vassiliou children:

> How dreadful it is ... that children are born of two parents, that they are the property of two parents with equal claim, that they do not spring fully grown from the brain, as Athena sprang from Zeus. What a ghastly mistake in evolution, for man to have attached such significance to identity, when he is condemned for survival to partition. (NE 284)

Psychological determinism then hovers uneasily between the effects of biological heredity and later influences, doubly determined when the parent also inculcates certain attitudes, as in Simon's case; he analyses his curiously unwilled marriage to Julie at some length with the aid of Freud and Proust: 'He really did think he could see it all now: he had been attracted to her because his life with his mother was so appalling' (*NE* 72). Even at the time he had offered to marry Julie, he knew he was provoking unhappiness for both of them, 'but there had seemed no possible choice. Inevitability had held him in its grip: psychological determinism had really got its claws into him' (*NE* 73).

Character, in its hereditary and environmentally moulded shape, is more important than chance in this plot. Unusually, the catastrophe that propels the plot forward towards the end of the narrative is not an accident, but a willed activity by Christopher, when, having taken his children out for Whitsun Saturday, according to his rights, he sends a telegram telling Rose he is taking the children away from her, out of the country.

A flurry of activity ensues, in which Rose, supported by Simon, takes out an injunction – with difficulty as it is a holiday – and then, informed by a phone call from Rose's resourceful eldest child Konstantin, they pursue the children to Rose's parents' country estate, where in fact Christopher has taken them. As his defiant gesture has caused the legal profession a great deal of unnecessary trouble, Christopher thereby loses all hope of putting up a good case for custody of his children, and is next heard of taking Simon's advice to return to live with Rose and his family. Drabble has prepared us for Rose's acceptance of this unpromising move by an earlier near breakdown on her part, when she almost convinces herself that she should renounce her rights with regard to the children in order to allow Christopher his parental rights and to avoid further stress.

In many ways, then, *The Needle's Eye* does fit into the genre of old-fashioned psychological novel, in that it concentrates on character, explores motives, avoids coincidence and accident, and makes sure its conclusion is happy but not too happy. Here the plot culminates in a set piece with the reunion of Rose and her children – as Simon looks on – at the intersection of two green avenues in the grounds of her parents' house, with an incongruous open day in aid of district nurses taking place in the background. This epiphanic reunion is a climax, and Simon finds it an artificial one:

The high green hedges froze in a crest, about to break: the smell of trodden grass surged and rose and surged again. The planned and geometric grandeur stiffened and oppressed him: it was too much, too much intended. He looked for cover. There was no cover. They were intended to walk, down the very centre, back to the house. (*NE* 326)

To balance this, the final few pages of the narrative extend into future years, showing that, as in *The Waterfall,* there is no 'conclusion', indicating the more desultory way in which life continues.

There is, however, still little comment from the narrator in this novel: some characters, such as Rose's friend Emily and her lover Meyer, are explained authoritatively, but most of the text is focalized through Simon, Rose or their friends. Drabble explains that she hoped here to have escaped from the one-character focus of her earlier works:

> I certainly was attempting to make Simon a whole person and to make Rose a whole person and to show these two whole people not comprehending each other wholly, and being surrounded by a lot of other people, whom they only partially comprehended, but who were hinted at, with degrees, as being real people.[3]

Indeed, the large amount of self-analysis offered by the characters, both in probing their feelings and in recollecting long episodes from the past, contributes to the static nature of some of the narrative. Drabble says the very long sentences of *The Needle's Eye* are there because of the complex subject matter:

> if you're trying to express what seemed to me some very complicated concepts, you're bound to get involved in your prose while you're doing it. Following it through is going to be a fairly painful, complicated process in itself. So presumably the reader goes through what I went through when I was writing it.[4]

It is not however the long sentences so much as the revisiting of material, as Simon and Rose circle round and restate their predicaments and their analyses of them, that gives the narrative a sense of slow progression. This static effect is quite unusual in the Drabble canon, where the early protagonists pressed on eagerly from one experience to another (or, like Jane Gray, diversified the monotony of her life story with changes of viewpoint and changes of direction), and the later novels cut from one scene to another with filmic abruptness. After this, characters were not allowed to be so self-indulgent; the more interventionist narrator was to add summary and criticism in larger amounts, expanding the focus to include not only the psychologically complex characters of the realist text, but also the processes of the narrative itself, as voiced by the organizing narrator.

6

I Do Not Care Very Much for Plots Myself (But I Do Like a Sequence of Events)

It was with apparent relief that Margaret Drabble had expanded her point of view in *The Needle's Eye* to two main centres of consciousness, with some insight into others. From the next novel, *The Realms of Gold*, onward, the role of the omniscient narrator increases and is used to place the characters' own narrative sections in perspective and in relation to each other. Looking back from 1990, Drabble said 'My principal linking device has been, increasingly, the use of the intrusive narrator, who bypasses the traditional narrative and speaks directly to the reader with a sort of immediate intimacy'.[1] Though speaking particularly of *The Radiant Way*, she added that she had used this method earlier, if not so extensively.

The Realms of Gold is, Margaret Drabble says, a comedy,[2] and as such the ironic tone of the narrator complements the reflections of the characters. Again the themes of heredity, upbringing and accident offer seductive answers to the questions about why things happen and why people are as they are. Heredity is a key element in *The Realms of Gold*, as the plot puts the question as to how far those with a similar heredity can make different choices and how far they can escape hereditary influence.

Most of the characters who are singled out for development are literally related: Frances Wingate, née Ollerenshaw, a successful archaeologist and divorced mother of four, is the major centre of consciousness, and is second cousin to Janet Bird, née Ollerenshaw, an isolated provincial housewife with a baby and an ineffectual but aggressive husband. Their cousin

51

David Ollerenshaw is a third, lesser figure in the novel. Occasional forays are also made into the minds of unrelated characters, most notably of Karel Schmidt, who is Frances's lover, and briefly into other lesser figures such as Janet's mother and the local solicitor.

Contrasts and similarities between these four main characters are reinforced by the comments of the narrator: for instance, Janet, as a young, insecure wife and mother is seen constantly pushing her pram around the unattractive, uninteresting local neighbourhood of Tockley, in contrast to Frances's more exotic busy life travelling to Italy and Africa. The presenting narrator draws attention to the management of the narrative, speaking of Janet as if she were a 'real' person:

> The fact that she was doing this, as she was some 23 pages ago does not indicate that no time has passed since that last brief encounter. Nor does it indicate a desire on the part of the narrator to impose an arbitrary order or significance upon events. It is simply a fact that Janet Bird spent a great deal of time pushing her pram up and down Tockley High Street. She had not much choice. She had little else to do. One could, arguably, have picked her up at one or another of the various monotonous and repetitive tasks that filled her day, but she might as well be allowed some exercise. For she gets little. (*RG* 127)

In a characteristic sequence, Janet is then seen as full of anxieties while preparing meticulously for a dinner party:

> However, her social doubts about the ordinary set were by now so profound that she used the Royal Worcester after all, giving herself the odd side plate ... If only there weren't any guests involved, she would be quite happy, setting tables. (*RG* 157)

And the narrator adds at this point an explicit contrast in a parenthesis about Frances:

> (Her second cousin Frances Wingate had always taken the opposite view. In the old days, when she had given dinner parties, she hadn't minded the guests; it was the bore of feeding them and setting tables for them to which she had objected. She never had anything that went with anything; all her sets were broken, and elderly professors or middle-aged stockbrokers were obliged to eat off children's plates decorated with pictures of Babar) (*RG* 157–8)

though this simple contrast is qualified by the note that 'Being, however, indirectly related to the heritage of Janet Bird née

Ollerenshaw, she hadn't felt quite as indifferent to these deficiencies as she might have done'(*RG* 158). The third-person omniscient narrator is able to add these modifying comments without putting all the burden of the self-analysis upon the character herself.

The digression about Frances is little more than half a page long, after which the story of Janet's dinner party continues: the brief interpolations continue to make links between the characters, as in an earlier transition between Janet reading about a battered baby, and Frances, 'reading of the same battering in the same paper at more or less the same hour, as she sat over a cup of coffee in her home at Putney', after which a further page of digression is introduced: 'David Ollerenshaw, while his cousins were indulging in the female pastimes of cups of coffee and afternoon naps, was making elaborate preparations for his trip to Adra' (*RG* 140). The narrative then again returns to Janet. Even Karel is briefly drawn into this sequence, when his views on Poles and Jews are contrasted to the romantic fantasies of Janet's library book.

In the context of Drabble's later novels it seems that the narrator is making a special point about experience: for human beings, the synchronicity of human experience is unimaginable – all the inhabitants of the earth at any given moment are coexisting, in such multiplicity that nobody can grasp more than a fraction of it at any one time. This contrast of huge numbers and individual experience recurs in Drabble's work. Yet the characters from time to time have a glimpse of the thick texture of human life, which is contributed to by coincidence and simultaneity. Frances feels the sense of connection and coexistence when she learns that David, a fellow delegate at the same conference in Africa, is her cousin, and another delegate 'proved to them that everybody was related to just about everybody, at remarkably few removes' (*RG* 266). The narrative method then tries to remind the reader of this simultaneity, though it is an effect impossible to convey completely satisfactorily in the verbal and linear medium of the novel.

As in other Drabble novels, these contrasts and juxtapositions seem to ask for some explanation. In spite of her confidence and success, Frances, the main character, first appears as someone who is caught in a double state of depression: initially and acutely she suffers a few hours of unmotivated, free-floating anguish, recurrent since her childhood; more chronically she is burdened by loneliness and misgivings about ageing and the future, prompted mainly by her own arbitrary rejection of Karel. As appropriate for one who knows she has brought about her own state of deprivation, Frances is inclined to blame individuals for their own difficulties. Her initial reaction to stories about misfortune is that 'These days, she blamed people for what happened to them, instead of excusing them' (*RG* 13) and she applies this, with a superficial kind of psychological determinism, to herself: 'It was partly her own fault that she was feeling so bad. She must, in some way, have wanted it. Otherwise, she wouldn't have come back to this very town, where she had parted from the only man she had ever loved ... She deserved to feel bad, after all'(*RG* 16).

Karel too comes to restrain his own fatal sympathy for the unfortunate. Reversing his position because of his own misery at the loss of Frances,

> he found himself changing into something quite different, he found himself blaming people, criticising them, noticing their least attractive features instead of their redeeming ones. When people were unhappy, he found himself thinking, it was invariably their own selfish fault. They got what they deserved. (*RG* 217)

Frances evolves some more tentatively psychological explications of her own and her family's state. Talking to her brother Hugh, she looks at her family and sees enough mental disturbance to make her own occasional troughs of despair seem unimportant:

> stories of the great-uncle who had hanged the cat and then himself, of the distant cousin who had thrown himself under a train, of aunts in lunatic asylums and another ancient cousin who had tramped the country preaching the word until he was found dead in a ditch. Some said murdered, though it was never known. (*RG* 102)

Her own younger sister had committed suicide, her brother Hugh is an alcoholic, and her father, the vice-chancellor of a new university and a distinguished biologist, has taken to staring blankly into space for hours at a time. She fears that Hugh's rather unstable son Stephen 'was suffering from some incurable and rat-like family disease, yet another manifestation of the same illness that had killed her sister, driven Hugh manic to the bottle and driven her father into a world of silent brooding' (*RG* 101). The 'rat-like' genetic explanation for destiny is limited here to a strong interest in recurrent family patterns of behaviour. Frances also favours explanations of destiny which take into account the environment, blaming 'Midlands sickness' for the Ollerenshaw instability.

In contrast to this, Frances, like Clara before her, also fitfully harbours a mystical belief in the power of the human mind to affect external events; her discovery of the site of an ancient North African city buried in the desert has been almost arbitrary, she thinks. On one level she can see it as a subconscious assembly of the evidence – 'the evidence was all there, it was simply that she alone had produced the correct interpretation of it all, and being correct, of course it had fitted' (*RG* 34) – but the way that she suddenly had glimpsed the truth 'with such conviction that it was like a revelation' continues to seem uncanny to her:

> I must be mad, she thought to herself. I imagine a city, and it exists. If I hadn't imagined it, it wouldn't have existed. All her life, things had been like that. She had imagined herself doing well at school, and had done well. Marrying, and had married. Bearing children, and had borne them. Being rich, and had become rich. Being free, and was free. Finding true love, and had found it. Losing it and had lost it. What next should she imagine? (*RG* 34–5)

This can in any case be explained as coincidence, which is used with some force in the plot. Frances's delayed reunion with Karel forms the spine of the narrative: Frances sends him a postcard from Italy, telling him she still loves him, at the beginning of the novel. This postcard is delayed by the Italian postal strikes for several months, causing her to think that Karel has decided to reject her in turn. She then mopes and waits until the much belated delivery of the postcard coincides with her own realization that the post is not, after all, infallible. The presenting narrator points to the similarities with *Tess of the D'Urbervilles*, though there Tess has pushed under the door, and, unknown to her, lost under the carpet, a letter confessing her sins, not a confession of love:

And to those who object to too much coincidence in fiction, perhaps one could point out that there is very little real coincidence in the postcard motif, though there are many other coincidences in this book. These days, the post being what it is, it would have been more of a miracle if the postcard had arrived on time, as Frances (unlike Tess of the D'Urbervilles) should have been sensible enough to realize, though (in this sense like Tess of the D'Urbervilles) her judgement too was clouded by emotion. (*RG* 224)

The climax of the narrative draws several threads together: Frances's great-aunt, a person vaguely mentioned in her childhood and otherwise unknown to her, has died of starvation in her remote midland cottage. A national Sunday newspaper has pounced on this example and is hounding Frances's parents, so that she hurriedly has to leave her conference in Africa in reply to their distraught telegrams. At this same conference, she has just met David Ollerenshaw and found that he is a cousin. And at the same time, her nephew Stephen and his baby daughter seem to have disappeared. Janet, who was the last person to see great-aunt Constance alive, is also drawn into the scandal, and at last meets her second cousin Frances. This is a drama which serves to bring the main characters together.

In the end, most of the people involved decide that Constance's death has not been tragic or anomalous: she chose to live in isolation in her old cottage in a rural, unspoilt corner of the countryside, and her death was in keeping with this choice. In spite of the more gruesome details of the dead woman's having eaten paper and cardboard in the last days of her starvation, the cottage and its garden are beautiful in their obliteration by the forces of nature, and so death in such a setting is seen as natural, and acceptable.

This Wordsworthian message – 'As in the eye of Nature he has liv'd,/ So in the eye of Nature let him die'[3] – however is a little too easy. Drabble has even stretched a point by making the cottage and its surroundings so beautiful in the flat wastes of Toxley, devoted otherwise to bare muddy acres of sugar beet. But Drabble follows her functional plot climax with a more stunning blow for the characters, in which Frances's missing nephew Stephen and his baby daughter are found dead, in a wood, where he has killed himself and his baby. Although they too have died in a natural setting, there is no sense of natural acceptability. The narrator gives Frances's thoughts in a powerful lament at the second funeral:

> This was the place: this was death. How can one make a friend of death, how can one accept graciously the wicked deal? It was better not to pretend. All ritual is a hollow mockery ... Nobody had felt the slightest desire to make matters better by burying Stephen in the Cotswolds churchyard, or even by alleviating this grim ceremony with some well-chosen words. Nobody cared, because they cared. Stephen was dead, and that was that. It was the thing, these days, to speak of making death less frightful, more dignified, more familiar. Perhaps there was something to be said for it. But for her part, she had drawn too far away from any human continuity to wish to know. Death and love. How dreadfully they contradict all culture, all process, all human effort. Stephen had been right. The silly curtains swished together, and Stephen and his child disappeared together into the red crater, made one with nature, transformed to black ash. (*RG* 351–2)

This is an abrupt and shocking transition from the almost pantheistic view of nature in the country churchyard to the harsher impersonal forces of mechanistic physical change, with which David is associated (we have seen him looking into a volcanic crater earlier in the novel), and the narrator authoritatively confirms that Frances here is thinking 'truly and bitterly' (*RG* 351).

Even so, Drabble does not close the novel with this funeral – hardly appropriate if it is in fact a comedy. Although this is the end of the main narrative sequence, it is as in *The Needle's Eye* followed by a transitional time bridge to a more distant period, which suggests that life must go on. What the narrator calls 'these projections' extend via 'the following days and weeks ... Gradually ... In the end ... over the years ... More years later ...' (*RG* 352–5). During this progression into the future Frances comes to terms with Stephen's death: 'perhaps it was not so bad. Perhaps, in some way, it was all right' (*RG* 353). This is an acceptance of his right, like Constance's, to die as he wished; it is also a recognition of the possible validity of his conclusion that life is not worth living, that living is worse than dying, which she suspects but avoids.

The comments on coincidence quoted above reflect the new assertiveness of the narrator which is to be characteristic of Drabble's fiction in the future. It might seem that the comic genre of the novel encourages both the use of coincidence and the narrator's joky intrusions, these being methods of drawing attention to the manipulation of the fiction by the author. There are in fact two dimensions of narrative comment here – the presenting narrator asserts that the characters and events are real, as did the first-person narrator in *The Waterfall*, and the organizing narrator recognizes that the characters and events are not real, are fictional, and can be manipulated. These two apparently contradictory positions are not as distinct as one might expect. For instance, the introductory pages to Part 3 of *The Realms of Gold* address the reader directly and refer to the mechanisms of narrating, but maintain the reality of the characters Janet and David:

> And that is enough, for the moment, of Janet Bird. More than enough, you might reasonably think, for her life is slow, even slower than its description, and her dinner party seemed to go on too long to her, as it did to you. Frances Wingate's life moves much faster. (Though it began rather slowly, in these pages – a tactical error, perhaps, and the idea of starting her off in a more manic moment has frequently suggested itself, but the reasons against such an opening are stronger, finally, than the reasons for it) ... We will return to Frances with relief: her diseases are meaningless and mild, her prognosis is good, she is a cheering spectacle, and should be given a fair chance. (Whether or not Janet Bird will be given a fair chance is another matter, as yet unresolved, and in the resolution, truth, likelihood, and a natural benevolence are at war.) But meanwhile, we must look briefly at David Ollerenshaw, the third of the Ollerenshaws, and I fear much the most impenetrable. I must confess that I had at this point intended to introduce him in greater depth ... On the other hand, he continues to exist, he has a significance that might one day become clear, and meanwhile he will have to speak, as it were, for himself. (*RG* 183–4)

All the three Ollerenshaws are presented as if 'real', but the parenthesis on Janet goes further, as does the mention of David's intended role, in emphasizing the organizing narrator's power to change the character's life, though 'truth' as opposed to 'likelihood' may imply some higher standard of faithfulness to real life. This power is flaunted jokingly before the reader as the narrator winds up the plot – 'So there you are. Invent a more suitable ending if you can ... A happy ending, you may say. Resent it if you like. She will not care: she is not listening' (*RG* 356).

The different functions of narration seem to be operating here without difficulty; possibly Margaret Drabble felt more liberated by the comic genre to begin using this flexible form, and we see the continuing interventions of the narrator, as a linking device, and as a marker of emphasis and importance, in the remaining novels, although the tone of the narrator's relationship with the reader may vary according to the nature of the narrative.

The Ice Age clearly cannot be described as a comedy, starting as it does with a series of catastrophes, and ending with the indefinite imprisonment of the main character in a remote Eastern European gaol. The number of actual and metaphorical prisons that appear in this novel throws into relief the concern for human freedom, particularly for individual free choice, and here it is again presented not so much in opposition to heredity but to accident and a sense of being coerced by large impersonal forces. The limitations of their individual circumstances freeze the characters into frustrating immobility, although the central image of the ice age refers mainly to the paralysis which the whole economic and political framework of society in the seventies imposes on the characters, as on the nation:

> A huge icy fist, with large cold fingers, was squeezing and chilling the people of Britain, that great and puissant nation, slowing down their blood, locking them into immobility, fixing them in a solid stasis, like fish in a frozen river: there they all were in their large houses and their small houses, with their first mortgages and second mortgages, in their rented flats and council flats and basement bedsits and their caravans: stuck, congealed, amongst possessions, in attitudes, in achievements they had hoped next month to shed and with which they were now condemned to live. The flow had ceased to flow; the ball had stopped rolling: the game of musical chairs was over. *Rien ne va plus,* the croupier had shouted. (*IA* 62–3)

This is not the view of a character; it is an example of the authoritative narrator, sketching in a depressing picture of Britain, but qualified with an ironic distance. *The Ice Age* follows the broad, multiple-stranded pattern developed in *The Realms of Gold*, but seems to extend further than its predecessor, partly because explicit reflections on the country as a whole are introduced, as in the paragraph just quoted.

Anthony Keating is the central character, and is stranded by a financial catastrophe, part of the general economic crisis, which has abruptly stopped the dealings of the property company of which he is co-director. Because he has recently had a mild heart attack, he is resting and avoiding stress in the large country house he has just bought in Yorkshire and which he probably will not be able to afford to keep. He asks himself 'how am I coping with my freedom, now I am freed from every institution, from school, from Oxford, from the BBC, from ITV, from all those restricting reassuring wombs?' (*IA* 119). But his withdrawal from all kinds of involvement, including the more recent excitements of property speculation, is not freedom, but lack of it.

Anthony is divorced and lives with beautiful Alison Murray, also divorced, who has given up her successful acting career to care for her younger daughter, Molly, a victim of cerebral palsy. When the novel opens, Alison's elder daughter, spoilt, sulky, adolescent Jane, is in a foreign prison awaiting trial for killing two people through dangerous driving. Also in prison is Anthony's close friend Len Wincobank, who has illegally moved money between different companies to keep his beleaguered enterprises afloat, and has received a gaol sentence as an example to others.

The plot of this novel is in outline an economic one, in the sense that the economic situation has a succession of effects on the main characters. Anthony is constricted by the immobility of his financial affairs: there is nothing he can do but wait while his partners try to stave off their debts and seek other purchasers for their huge, unsold, unsaleable real-estate package; on a smaller scale, he is still paying for a mortgage on his previous unsold, unsaleable house in London. Also, on his doctor's orders he has to refrain from consoling himself with drink, cigarettes and sex, another restriction of choice. Even Alison is absent as the novel opens, trying to do something to help Jane, in the fictional country Drabble has called Walachia.

Anthony wrestles with his predicament for two thirds of the novel and gradually his financial situation becomes a little less ice-bound: eventually, the deal which they had been involved in, and for which they owe enormous sums of money, is concluded satisfactorily. At the same time, he manages to sell his old house, and after settling all his large debts and double mortgage, finds he is just about solvent – he has four thousand pounds in the bank, no debts and no job. And his doctor tells him that he is looking well, and that he had not really been expected to give up smoking and drinking. At all this good news, Anthony feels not relieved but 'deeply aggrieved' (*IA* 218):

> Yet again, he was going to have to decide what to do with his life. It was too exhausting. It was too much of an effort. He wished that somebody would throw a bomb through the pub window and put him out of his misery. He did not know what he thought about anything: why should he be expected to go on making up his mind? The problems were too complex. He had neither the intelligence nor the perseverance to solve them. On the other hand, he was quite well aware that he had too much intelligence and too much perseverance to give up the struggle. He had no choice but to go on making choices. (*IA* 219)

The pressures of freedom are shown as just as disruptive as the icy grip of inaction. After the better financial news, he goes through a period of mental turmoil, drinking himself into a state of mania every day. In her turn, Alison emerges from her own depression, but considers leaving him: his present solvency and bad behaviour 'left her curiously free, to think again, to reconsider ... Like Anthony, she wished at times that she had not been presented with this sudden freedom of choice' (*IA* 225).

The plot here takes a sudden new direction: as in earlier Drabble novels, a crisis erupts which breaks the stasis of Anthony's predicament, for while Alison is away visiting Molly, the Foreign Office suggests that Anthony should fly to Walachia where Jane is unexpectedly about to be released, in case she is forgotten or re-imprisoned in the course of a threatening revolution. This is the point where Anthony's luck in avoiding the death and imprisonment which have struck so many of his friends and colleagues abruptly ends. There is indeed a revolution, and while Jane is allowed to set off with Anthony, at the very embarkation gate his passport is taken away, though Jane retains hers. Jane escapes on the last plane out of the country, but Anthony disappears from the narrative for a while. Believed dead, he is eventually heard of as imprisoned. Here the novel leaves him, apparently resigned to his fate, writing a book on the 'nature of God and the possibility of religious faith' (*IA* 285).

This conclusion surprises his friends, for, as Alison recalls, she has never known Anthony refer to God at all, apart from swearing, and the narrative has made plain that as a son of a clergyman he has reacted against his father's beliefs – 'the denial of his father and all his father had expected of him' (*IA* 19). Yet the thought comes to him unbidden on the hot dusty road up to Jane's prison: 'I do not know how man can do without God.' As the narrator points out, this is both like and unlike the miraculous conversion of Saint Paul: 'like Paul on the way to Damascus: not exactly felled by realisation, for alas, faith had not accompanied the concept. But it stopped him in his tracks, nevertheless' (*IA* 258). This paves the way for his later meditations, while shut up in the Walachian prison camp:

> If God did not appoint this trial for me, then how could it be that I should be asked to endure it, he asks. He cannot bring himself to believe in the random malice of the fates, those three grey sisters. He is determined, alone, to justify the ways of God to man. (*IA* 285–6)

Alison Murray, on the other hand, has always felt that the random malice of the fates – accident, in short – would be a better explanation for life. For her, the alternative explanation would be the power of the human will to direct destiny, and she dreads the implications of responsibility and guilt. While reflecting on the illness of her hostile elder sister Rosemary, who has had her breast removed because of a malignant growth, she questions the simple view of human choices:

> She glimpsed for a moment, in the dark night, a primitive causality so shocking, so uncanny, that she shivered and froze. A world where the will was potent, not impotent: where it made, indeed, bad choices, and killed others by them, killed them, deformed them, destroyed them.
>
> I gave Rosemary cancer of the breast, said Alison to herself, aloud, to see how the words sounded. They did not sound very foolish. (*IA* 97)

Later she associates this primitive causality with both poetic justice and modern psychology:

> She had been so scornful, when younger, of those who thought all illnesses psychosomatic, those who talked of 'cancer types' ... Nowadays, she was not so sure. As one grows older, as one explores, slowly, the responses of mind and body, one learns a respect for

their intimate connections. There is no such thing as an accident. We are all marked down. We choose what our own ill thoughts choose for us. (*IA* 152)

This is the dark side of Frances Wingate's impression that she has willed the mainly beneficial achievements of her life: if one believes that everything is caused by the human will, then someone has to be blamed for all the suffering in human life, for instance Molly's mental limitations and frustration. It is to avoid such unbearable chains of responsibility and liability that Alison tries to sustain her belief in accident. She does not wish to apportion blame: 'For years, for ten years, Alison had striven to believe in accidents, in the possibility of bad luck, for that would exonerate herself, her husband, Jane, Rosemary, her parents – they would all be exonerated by such a belief from the guilt of Molly's sacrifice' (*IA* 97). Alison feels that it is better to be able to blame accident than to have to blame another human being – especially oneself.

The theme of accident and coincidence is also followed through the experiences of Len Wincobank, the young property developer of working-class origins who had first introduced Anthony to 'the excitement and romance of the business' (*IA* 27). Len has accepted his imprisonment as accident, an example of bad luck – he happened to be useful to make into an example and satisfy public hostility to property speculators. But a fellow prisoner, Callendar, more seriously involved in business malpractice, has a more spectacular explanation. He tells Len portentously that 'something has gone wrong with the laws of chance' (*IA* 162). He links together confusedly the fates of his acquaintances, the rate of inflation and his last night's selection of cards while playing bridge. Len shrewdly defines this as Callendar's attempt to find an excuse for himself in all the catastrophes that have affected him and his circle.

These views, supported by such bizarre examples, seem offered up for ridicule, yet they clearly relate to the situation and plot development of the novel as a whole. The 'icy fist' of the quotation above represents the economic crisis which has put pressure on business deals everywhere, causing the collapse of companies like Anthony's, Len's and Callendar's. At the same time, this was a period of extremism in the conflict in Northern Ireland, and activists were running a bombing campaign in England, to put pressure on public opinion and the government. Drabble reminds the reader of this through the story of Kitty Friedmann, a peripheral character, whose husband Max has been killed by a terrorist bomb, thrown at the restaurant where they were celebrating their ruby wedding anniversary. In the blast, Kitty has also been injured, and has lost a foot. This had been 'an Irish bomb', with no connection direct or indirect with the Jewish Max and Kitty: 'The whole thing had been a ghastly, arbitrary accident. The bomb simply happened to have blown up Max and Kitty, a random target. This past year had been so full of accidents that they had begun to seem almost normal' (*IA* 11).

Anthony's heart attack, at the unusually young age of 38, when he had been extremely fit and athletic, is another unpredictable accident, and Jane Murray, who, as her mother considers, 'could drive perfectly well, had chosen to kill two men in the country which possessed the most stringent penalties for traffic offences in Europe'(*IA* 97). Callendar's theory of the laws of chance breaking down is based, the narrator tells us, on his reading of Arthur Koestler's *The Roots of Coincidence*,[4] a book that toys with the idea that clusters of accidents are drawn together as with the attraction of subatomic particles. Independently, Anthony is struck by a similar image of his own afflictions, which are 'too severe, too sudden, too dramatic. It was as though he had strayed into some charged field, where death and disaster became commonplace ... They were attracted to him, they leapt towards him like iron filings to a magnet, they clustered eagerly around him' (*IA* 18).

The accidents detailed above are not all, however, the completely random events that their victims and observers sometimes think them. The economic situation is all too logical in its development, as Len tries to explain to Callendar. The Irish conflict is also part of a traceable development, and has economic as well as religious and political roots. Although physically healthy, Anthony has been under intense stress because of the financial crisis, and we learn later that his mother has a weak heart, and his heart attack may have had strong hereditary influence. So although these accidents, chronicled at the beginning of the novel, may indeed have 'no one common cause' (*IA* 12), there is a general dependence on the malaise of the capitalist system, and their separate causes are logical.

The accidents that so baffle the characters force them to look at their choices: surprisingly, such freedom of choice does not seem to be acceptable to them. Anthony's summons by Clegg is preceded by an idyllic episode when Anthony and Alison, recovered from their various mental turmoil, consider thoughtfully and at leisure what to do with their lives in the future. Such rational planning and considered choices are not, it seems, the way that life proceeds – Humphrey Clegg intervenes, the Wallachian revolution intervenes, and Anthony instead finds himself in a remote foreign prison camp. He later tells his visitor from the embassy 'There's something rather consoling about the lack of options. Freedom is a mixed blessing, don't you sometimes think?' (*IA* 284).

Anthony's solution to the problem of living, then, is to investigate the role of God in human life: 'He cannot evade the idea that God has given him the chance to work out the first causes and last causes, and that he must not reject it' (*IA* 285), the narrator tells us. This is therefore a religious answer to the problem of the accidents and coincidences experienced by the characters and their society, but at the same time it is hedged and modified by layers of provisionality. The narrator reminds us through Anthony's own disclaimer that his interest in God 'may be due simply to his peculiar situation' and that he has little else to occupy his mind at this point.

By contrast with *The Ice Age*, *The Middle Ground* is an extreme case of the 'plotless' novel, in that the process of change in its main character develops slowly and without crises – Drabble remarked that 'Writing the blurb was a nightmare, because nothing really happens in it at all'.[5] Like *A Summer Bird-Cage*, the novel refers from time to time to 'the year' in its protagonist's life, but in fact it is limited in its nominal time-scheme to October, November, and perhaps part of December. These few months are, however, merely the platform for a flourishing growth of reminiscences and associative digressions, so that the lives of the main characters are laid before us, sometimes in summary but often in extensive anecdotal detail. This is necessarily the case, as the main theme of the two-month narrative scheme is a mid-life reassessment by the protagonist, Kate Armstrong.

Like Anthony Keating in the early part of *The Ice Age*, Kate is held in a kind of suspension, waiting for the next thing, but she is not to be struck down by any sudden blow of fate as Anthony was. Like Anthony, Kate has already suffered a plentiful series of blows, and Drabble shows how she has to come to terms with the stage of her life that she has reached, without the dramatic assistance of the foreign revolution and prison camp that were forced upon Anthony.

Although Kate is the main character, her experiences are paralleled or contrasted with those of her friends and acquaintances, all of whom live closely linked lives in London – this is, says Drabble, 'about the state of London rather than the state of Britain. It's very much a London novel. It's got no plot; it's very much a texture novel'.[6] Drabble points out that the party episode that concludes the novel is based on the party at the end of Virginia Woolf's *Mrs Dalloway*, which Kate's daughter is studying for A level (this is a 'literary joke').[7] Another comparison can be made to Angus Wilson's *The Middle Age of Mrs Eliot*, a novel Drabble admires, where Mrs Eliot's disastrous excursions into society parallel the series of appalling lovers Kate tries out at this period. *The Middle Ground*, then, is a novel in the recognized sub-genre of mid-life reassessment, as its title suggests, and one of the main features of such a subject is the sense of alienation from normal life, which otherwise carries the individual along without time to question any experiences. This alienation is interestingly reflected in the philosophy of life of Kate's friend Hugo. He was influenced in his childhood by writings about the East, and now is insidiously tempted to gain peace by detaching himself from life – as Anthony did? – but this is implied to be unsatisfactory, an option which Kate has to reject.

Memories of the past, drawn from the minds of all the characters, are interspersed with glimpses of the present. Kate is first seen discussing her problems with Hugo over lunch. Then the presenting narrator, rejecting any artistic transition, baldly announces 'Here is an account of Kate's past history, some, if not all, of which must have led her to wherever she is' (*MG* 17) (even the 'must have' and 'wherever' disclaim omniscient insight), and gives a biography of Kate which lasts for sixty pages before getting back to the situation she is now in.

This biography describes Kate's childhood in Romley, a dismal, depressed area on the eastern fringes of London, and her relationship with her dogmatic, opinionated father and large, limp, agoraphobic mother; she claims to have escaped their abnormal influence unscathed, but her brother Peter was less fortunate, growing from a fat unpopular child to a fat unpopular adolescent, pushed into unsuitable, overtaxing middle-class management jobs. Kate dominated her secondary modern school contemporaries, thanks to her histrionic prowess in telling shocking stories to a gasping audience of her schoolfriends, which could be seen as some kind of apprenticeship for her later unexpected rise from suburban, unqualified photographer's assistant to success and fame as a journalist. It is at the bohemian house of one Hunt, apparently a dealer in second-hand goods and antiques, that Kate meets her future husband, the painter Stuart Armstrong, whose cosmopolitan family adopt Kate and teach her new attitudes and skills.

Although in middle age Kate is beginning to feel insecure about her writing abilities, it is her personal life which has plunged her into a gloomy reappraisal. After having three children with what she considered inadequate support from Stuart, she divorces him and begins a long affair with Ted Stennett, husband of her close friend Evelyn. (Evelyn, disillusioned by Ted's affairs with other women, is not too worried about it, and even seems glad to have Ted's attentions directed away from home.) However, after a few complacent years Kate begins to feel uneasy: her eldest son leaves home, her confidence in her work is faltering, and she realizes things can't go on like this for ever:

> A vague anxiety began to invade her complacency ... She began to regret her lack of formal education. She enrolled for evening classes, but never had time to attend them. She envied colleagues who had had the sense to pull out and take degree courses in politics, economics, sociology; she was too old, too ignorant and too successful to imitate them. (*MG* 59)

All this is in the recent past, and we learn in flashbacks that, during this period of stress, her relationship with Ted has collapsed in bitterness and hurt, as she finds that he has started another affair with an anonymous 'woman in Cambridge'. What

Ted does not know is that Kate has just become pregnant by him, has at first decided to keep the baby to give herself a sense of purpose, but has found that the foetus is afflicted with spina bifida. After a further struggle with herself, she has an abortion, but loses all her remaining confidence. The series of brief and dreadful relationships with horrible men follows, and upon finally shaking these off, she finds herself in the dreary state of calm with which the novel opens.

The biography of Kate takes up over a fifth of the novel, though it also includes briefer biographies of Ted and Evelyn, with a few peripheral anecdotes developed at some length, and the presenting narrator concludes it with 'This was last month, the month before the encounter with Hugo with which we opened this history' (*MG* 81). The reader expects some new plot line to open at this point, but there is no strong plot development, although two current situations are immediately mentioned – that Kate is working on a television film about women and the choices they make as school-leavers, and that she has taken in as a lodger Mujid, an Iraqi refugee, a connection of a Lebanese acquaintance. The former situation leads us back to Kate's childhood, as she interviews staff and former pupils at Romley Fourways, her own old school, and the latter expands Kate's world outwards somewhat, as she struggles to cope with Mujid's outsider's point of view.

The central part of the novel, for about another quarter of its length, is mainly taken up with Kate's excursion back to Romley, unvisited since her parents left the area, where she delves into her memories of the past. Like several other Drabble heroines, she goes back to her roots and presses for an answer; but where Rose, Clara and Liz find memories or even hard evidence of their hereditary or environmental shaping, Kate at first denies any such discovery. As the narrator comments,

> The middle years, caught between children and parents, free of neither: the past stretches back too densely, it is too thickly populated, the future has not yet thinned out. No wonder a pattern is slow to emerge from such a thick clutter of cross-references, from such trivia, from such serious but hidden connections. (*MG* 182)

At this point, however, certain moments of reconciliation and renewal, possibly even of 'pattern', begin to appear. There are three notable positive insights in the next section of plot: first, Kate finds a book of Russian fairy stories, not in the drawers and cupboards of her old home, but in the school book cupboard. Reflection on her childhood has driven Kate to feel that somehow her relationship with her brother Peter is significant – she wonders whether her aggressiveness and her refusal to compete in scholarly success, instead of protecting him, in fact isolated him and left him open to others' criticism. Did this lay down the template for her doomed relationship with Stuart? She astutely interprets the Russian fairy tale, about a sister and a brother, as depicting two sides of her own character: the heroine is a protective, caring sister, but there is also a wicked old toothless witch, a doppelgänger who takes her place and tries to kill the little brother. So Kate, in seeming to protect, has climbed to success and safety by rejecting her brother and her husband.

A second moment of insight occurs to Kate as she comes back from another interview. Ruminating on the varied lives she is investigating, she thinks 'How quite extraordinarily odd people are and how interesting and how diverse, and how lucky I am, how astonishingly lucky, to be able to listen to them all, and how I love my job' (*MG* 193). This moment of engagement and renewed positive energy seems the beginning of revival for Kate – after all, she is interested in people, and she does love her job, even if she will have to move on.

This period comes to a close with firm narratorial intervention saying 'This document began in October, with Kate and Hugo at lunch. During November, the following events took place ...' (*MG* 210), and indeed a list of events follows, including Hugo writing another chapter of his book, Mujid buying a pair of Clark's shoes, various strikes starting and stopping. The picture is of multifarious London life, and the life of Britain beyond that, continuing simultaneously as before.

What seems at first to be one more item on this list of incidents is the conclusion of Kate's TV film about women, but description of the film develops into a lengthy sequence that eventually leads to the main violent crisis of the novel. Kate and the director[8] have asked Hugo to watch the first unedited versions of the filmed interviews, and after lunch, when the friends separate, the third epiphany is granted to Kate: she goes somewhat self-consciously to look at paintings in the National

Gallery. As she looks at the depiction by Claude Lorraine of *Psyche locked out of the Palace of Cupid*, she is struck by the freedom that the sulky Psyche ought to be enjoying – 'the sea, and little white sails free in the wind, in the sunlight … The castle of love was a prison, a fortress, a tomb, how could she not appreciate her luck in being locked out, in being safe here in the open air? Let her rise and go' (*MG* 218).

This is not a simple recipe for happiness that Kate can directly apply to her own situation: she is quite aware of the fascination of erotic love. The point is rather that acceptance of its loss can be borne, and has its compensations, Kate thinks. It reinforces the lesson of the dreadful lovers, and the ability to 'rise and go' echoes the opening of the Russian fairy tale that had so caught Kate's imagination: 'How extraordinary was the opening of the story, the brother and sister setting out to walk through the whole of the wide world. But where else could one go, but through the whole world?' (*MG* 160). In the end, Kate has to embrace her freedom, and continue with confidence.

An abrupt change of narrative focus to Suzannah, Hugo's daughter, on her way late the same evening to stay with her friends, the children of Ted and Evelyn Stennett, makes a transition to the only crisis in the novel, for Evelyn has been caught up in a fight at the house of one of her clients, and has had chemical cleaning fluid thrown in her face, with damaging effect on her eyes. Luckily Evelyn has been able to put her face under the tap quite quickly, and is being treated in hospital, but her brush with violence has a sobering effect on her family and friends.

Evelyn is a more important character in the novel than Hugo, as she provides a continuing, sometimes consciously evoked contrast with Kate. Kate feels that Evelyn is a 'real woman', fulfilling what is expected of her efficiently. In the late twentieth century, a 'real woman', at least a well-educated one, is not expected to stay at home: Evelyn works in a traditional women's caring profession as a social worker, then comes home to cook – her daughter Vicky seeing her mother falling asleep in her chair after dinner as the guests chat, vows 'never will I let myself become a slave to convention, never will I marry and cook dinners and wear myself out trying to do too many things at once' (*MG* 209). This comment emphasizes the negative side of

Evelyn's success as a 'real woman'. But as a clever, thoughtful woman she helps to articulate the philosophical ideas of the novel, and has urged upon the younger generation of her children and her friends' children the need to act confidently, and that 'cities were made safe only by a conspiracy of faith' (*MG* 219).

Clearly, however, it would be naïve to suppose good faith warded off all evil, and Evelyn's stoical confidence indicates instead the more limited consolation that even when evil strikes, people can still survive. Visiting her in hospital, Kate looks out over the view of London, in a passage which draws together the three major insights she has achieved during the last sequence of the narrative – a hint of advice to Psyche, sense of release from the mythic family-based pattern of the past, and the positive elements of her attitude to life:

> London, how could one ever be tired of it? How could one stumble dully through its streets, or waste time sitting in a heap staring at a wall? When there it lay, its old intensity restored, shining with invitation, all its shaggy grime lost in perspective, imperceptible from this dizzy height, its connections clear, its pathways revealed. The city, the kingdom. The aerial view. Kate gazed east towards Romley. The little sister is resurrected, dug up, dragged from the river, the stone that weighted her dissolves, she rises up. Perhaps, perhaps, thought Kate ... The aerial view of human love, where all connections are made known, where all roads connect? (*MG* 238)

At this point, Kate, as if released from the curse that has held her down during this unhappy year, tells Evelyn she will celebrate with a party, a party to unite the numbers of people who make up her life.

In this novel, the narrator has been a guide rather than a confidante, and the systematic marking of transitions and phases in the novel have tended towards the management function of the organizing narrator; this has emphasized the excursions into past time, with longer developments in the present as the narrative unfolds. The presenting narrator often uses an ironic tone, with her 'busy Kate, comical Kate' implying some insincerity and theatricality on Kate's part, but also describes Kate's bewilderment and desperation from an omniscient point of view. Kate is observed and compared with other characters, such as Hugo and Evelyn, but it is worth noting also the role of Mujid: he has little to do but challenge Kate's conscience from time to time, but he is also a shadowy observer of the western way of life in which he has taken refuge. His innocent eye questions the behaviour of the British people who surge around him in this city. The perspective of these other, critical eyes asks why the shape of society is as it is.

7

Reading the Plot of the Past

The Radiant Way is the first of three linked novels (the others being *A Natural Curiosity* and *The Gates of Ivory*) which together, unusually for Margaret Drabble, cover the whole decade of the 1980s and incorporate extensive time lapses in their unfolding – unlike the tight time-schemes of the early novels.

Although the narrator calls her narrative 'this non-story' (*RW* 301), in fact there are far more dramatic plot events in *The Radiant Way* than in *The Middle Ground*. The central characters are Liz Headleand, Alix Bowen and Esther Breuer, who met as undergraduates at Cambridge: the main focus is on Liz and Alix, while Esther, an art historian of solitary and eccentric private life, is less fully developed, and indeed the character of Liz's sister Shirley is at least as well established as Esther's. Expanding outward from this nucleus is a vast range of characters, almost all of a comfortable middle-class status, and including a number of people active in the media, not only because of the trio's Cambridge friends who have gone into theatre and television, but because Liz's husband Charles is a television producer. This is a novel which exploits its huge cast of characters to point to coincidences and links, as seen in *The Realms of Gold* and *The Ice Age*, sometimes ironically, sometimes with more serious intent.

The sense of connections between different strands of life, emphasized in earlier novels, is particularly felt by Alix, who works, as many women do, at insecure, underpaid part-time jobs in education and administration. As she travels across the suburbs of London, she reflects upon the multiplicity of human lives lived cheek by jowl across the city and across the country, much as Kate Armstrong had recognized the intricate proximity of lives packed together in her part of London:

She aspired to a more comprehensive vision. She aspired to make connections. She and Liz, over supper together, often spoke of such things. Their own stories had strangely interlocked, and sometimes she had a sense that such interlockings were part of a vaster network, that there was a pattern, if only one could discern it, a pattern that linked these semi-detached houses of Wanley with those in Leeds and Northam, a pattern that linked Liz's vast house on Harley Street with the Garfield Centre towards which she now herself drove. The social structure greatly interested Alix. She had once thought of herself as unique, had been encouraged (in theory at least) by her education and by her reading to believe in the individual self, the individual soul, but as she grew older she increasingly questioned these concepts: seeing people perhaps more as flickering impermanent points of light irradiating stretches, intersections, threads, of a vast web, a vast network, which was humanity itself: a web of which much remained dark, apparently but not necessarily unpeopled: peopled by the dark, the unlit, the dim spirits, as yet unknown, the past and the future, the dead, the unborn, and herself, and Brian, and Liz, and Charles, and Esther, and Teddy Lazenby, and Otto and Caroline Werner, and all the rest of them at that bright party, and in these discreet anonymous dark curtained avenues and crescents were but chance and fitful illuminations, chance meetings, chance and unchosen representatives of the thing itself. We are all but a part of a whole which has its own, its distinct, its other meaning: we are not ourselves, we are crossroads, meeting places, points on a curve, we cannot exist independently for we are nothing but signs, conjunctions, aggregations. (*RW* 72–3)

These are only Alix's theories, as the narrator makes clear by noting the possibility that she may have personal reasons for thinking this way. Alix married directly after graduating, had a baby nine months later, and a few months after that, Sebastian, her attractive, rather weak husband, was drowned in a swimming pool, leaving her struggling in poverty to care for baby Nicholas. Over the years, Alix managed to survive, by dint of part-time work, until she married Brian Bowen, with whom she has a second son, Sam. As the novel opens, she teaches English in a women's prison on one or two evenings, and spends three days a week working for an obscure unit of the Home Office near Piccadilly. She thus has met a wide range of people, from the celebrated artists who were friends of Sebastian's talented and well-known parents, to the tramps befriended on her aimless, pram-pushing walks in the time of her poverty.

The theme of patterns and networks may, however, be an illusion, as it proves for Liz at the beginning of the narrative. Liz, unlike Alix, is very prosperous – lengthy training, first as a doctor, then as a psychiatrist, has prepared her for success in her profession, and after a brief and stormy marriage to Edgar Lintot she has married Charles Headleand, widower with three small sons, and pursued a busy, hectic career parallel to his career in television, during which she successfully brings up her three stepsons and produces two daughters of her own. The passage of time is marked as important from the first: the novel opens as 1979 gives way to 1980, with the Headleands holding a New Year's Eve party. Liz, perhaps naturally as the hostess of this large gathering, has a sense of controlling patterns: 'here, under this roof, at her command, patterns would form, and dissolve and form again ... The dance would be to her tune' (RW 8); she sees the party as a celebration of surviving twenty years of marriage, 'as a sign that they had weathered so much and were now entering a new phase' (RW 6), and as marking Charles's move to New York, where she intends to visit but not to join him. She also looks forward to the unexpected, having felt that too much is becoming predictable in her life, that she knows too much about everything.

All this is highly ironic, as during the party Liz's realization gradually crystallizes that Charles is in fact going to divorce her. The maturity and tolerance of their marriage, which she has supposed they were celebrating, is revealed as a state of detachment and disagreement, only tolerable because they hardly see anything of each other. Charles wants to marry Lady Henrietta Latchett, a predatory socialite who will entertain for him and accompany him as Liz has never been prepared to do. Naturally, Liz's confidence in being able to see and control patterns is shattered.

The Liz part of the narrative is similar to the material Drabble had been writing about in her previous few novels, but other parts of the novel are more sensational and spectacular even than the bombing and revolution seen in *The Ice Age*. It is Alix and Esther who are involved in these other dramatic plot strands. Esther's more muted life is devoted to research into details of art history, which she seldom publishes, supported thinly by lecturing and reviewing; but she has for years been in love with the married Italian academic Claudio Volpe, who has an obsession with werewolves and associated witchcraft. Esther reveals to Liz some of her concerns about Claudio, who is now causing uproar in Italy by openly discussing his supposed encounters with the supernatural; Liz confirms Esther's decision to detach herself gradually from Claudio, who, perhaps subconsciously realizing this loss of support, becomes ill and dies. Drabble says that the Claudio plot was 'my little joke about magic realism, a sort of response to it. I'm interested in the way the irrational fits into the rational world',[1] and there is a gothic line of connection between this and the series of murders being perpetrated in the area where Esther lives. At rather distant intervals in the narrative, there is mention of a serial killer in west London, dubbed the Horror of Harrow Road; women, usually black women, are found around the Harrow Road area, murdered, and the last few with their heads cut off. Esther at first is unaware, she claims, of this murder story, but her anxieties about Claudio take on a strange congruence with the murder pattern, as she dreams of a severed head (Claudio's?) addressing her from the canal towpath.

Meanwhile Alix is involved, not with witchcraft, but with crime, because of her teaching work in the prison, where Jilly Fox, who has committed various robbery and drug offences and tried to kill her father, has become attached to her. After Jilly is released, Alix reluctantly agrees to visit her one winter afternoon, at a squat in west London, close to the Harrow Road. Jilly claims to be waiting for the end, and resists all Alix's sensible advice and suggestions. Because her car has been vandalized and immobilized during her brief visit, Alix has to return the next day: her car, surrounded by police, now contains the severed head of Jilly Fox.

Some time later, Alix and Liz are spending the evening at Esther's flat, as they often do, and become aware of mysterious police activity in the neighbourhood. The police are in fact closing in on the flat above Esther's, where her neighbour, the 'quiet young man' who has lived there for many years, is arrested and later charged with the Harrow Road murders.

These events then are less like the patterns and networks of human society than the coincidences of a carefully planned plot. Another set of patterns involves the recurrence of the names of the related and distinguished Stocklinch, Hestercombe and Oxenholme families, whose crest and initials decorate a wine-cooler mysteriously standing in Liz's mother's house: this is preparation for further plot complications in the next part of the trilogy.

At another level however, the links and coincidences continue to have significance in themselves. Alix's husband Brian comes from Liz's home town, the Northam encountered in earlier Drabble novels, and his father is Liz's sister Shirley's sister-in-law's uncle by marriage, a relationship which has no other plot repercussions. The narrator describes Alix's confusion about this: 'was this perhaps not odd at all? Alix was not sufficiently numerate to be able to calculate the odds against such an apparently odd relationship, though she could not help but feel that its component, accidental parts were startlingly combined'; and Alix also adds incidentally that her friend Otto Werner's wife Caroline was a cousin of Liz's first husband (*RW* 73). Several other such links are offered in the course of the novel, such as the narrator's information that Otto's father had danced with Esther's mother in pre-war Vienna, 'but neither of them remembers the incident, and therefore, perhaps, it does not exist?' (*RW* 74). (This recalls Frances Wingate being told that all western Europeans are related 'within remarkably few removes' (*RG* 266).) Naturally, to some extent the characters move in similar circles, and so they meet people with whom they have connections – as Esther is leaving her flat to fly to Rome, she unknowingly passes the doomed Jilly Fox in the street, and meets Stephen Cox, a constant traveller, already known to her as a close friend of Alix, Brian and Liz, in the airport lounge. But overall, the implication of the encounters and coincidences seems to return to the theme that human life is multifarious and more interconnected than we realize.

Playfully the novel also refers to several of the characters from previous Drabble novels, just as in *The Middle Ground* Gabriel Denham from *Jerusalem the Golden* and Rosamund Stacey from *The Millstone* briefly reappear: at Liz's party, Kate Armstrong herself appears, as does her ex-lover Ted Stennett, and even

Anthony Keating from *The Ice Age*, now released from the foreign prison camp and a friend of Liz. Parenthetically we later hear that 'Kate Armstrong's one-time lodger, Mujid, was injured by a shell, but not seriously' (*RW* 229). Others are to appear later in the trilogy. These are jokes, but it reinforces Alix's theory that interlockings are a significant part of the network of humanity, and may even imply that such connections to one's fellow creatures perhaps should entail some sense of responsibility for them.

The lengthy time-scheme emphasizes the exceptional deterioration of society not only in Britain but throughout the world: time passes and things do not improve; Liz's promise to visit her mother is delayed for three and a half years, and the narrator tells us: 'These were the years of inner city riots, of race riots in Brixton and Toxteth' (*RW* 227) and 'During these years, war continued to rage between Iraq and Iran, but the West did not pay much attention' (*RW* 229).

It is Alix, always the most politically conscious of the three friends, who seeks a meaning for the apparently random weave of life by proposing a political interpretation. She has become less radical in her own political beliefs, and now diverges from the still radical Brian, because of her disillusion with the good will and common sense in the public in general. Near the end of the novel, Alix subjects herself to a lengthy interrogation, where she probes her own distrust of people, concern about the deterioration of society and pessimism about its further inevitable decline. The decade's economic pressures and obsession with productivity are to result in the closure of Brian's college department and in his losing his job, and Alix tries to understand how these apparently unexpected catastrophes can happen:

> She put them one beside another, like building blocks: National Service, Jury Service, Men, Women, Manual Work, Fear, Picket Lines, the Royal Family, Social Class, Adult Education. Patiently she lined them up. Unlike Liz, she was patient. They made no sense, these blocks, they did not make a building, but she would continue, patiently, persistently, to line them up and to look at them. To rearrange them. She would compel them: or if she failed to compel them, it would not be through want of effort. (*RW* 170–1)

Drabble's narrative is doing the same sort of rearranging and building. From a social point of view the novel does not offer a positive programme; it has been accused of being pessimistic, and Drabble replies: 'Yes, it was meant to be. I am depressed; we ought to have got a bit further by now. I see a terrible failure of nerve in the political and educational system.'[2]

She was anxious for her novel to be read seriously:

> I'd like to think *The Radiant Way* is an important book. It's not prophetic, I'm recording, and I think that can be useful. An important role for a writer is simply to use your eyes and tell the truth. I also think there is a moral basis to my work – though I feel more tentative about saying this ... But I do write from a sense of the worth of all human beings, which I hope comes through in the book.[3]

The social framework is not the only influence upon the characters. Other explanations include the effects of heredity. Liz, like the protagonists of earlier Drabble novels, has a grim, repressive, reclusive mother, one who had inflicted even more deprivation and lack of affection on Liz and her sister Shirley than her avatars in the preceding novels. Liz escaped through education, as Clara had done, and feels, as Clara had, that there had been some kind of disappointment which had laid waste her mother's family life.

Liz specializes in the psychological problems of adopted children when reunited with their natural parents, a field she may have taken up because of her own fatherless situation: 'The real mother had been there, solidly absent, a constant and insoluble distress, a damaged being, a victim, a mystery. Too painful, too inexplicable to contemplate. So Liz, as a child, had contemplated her missing father instead' (*RW* 138). After their mother's death, Liz and Shirley find something more than Clara Maugham had done: their father, whom they had thought to have died in the war, soon after Shirley's birth, in fact had been accused of child molestation and, though acquitted, had committed suicide. Liz, as a psychiatrist, had been suspicious of her own buried knowledge of some such scandal, in her strangely blank memories of her first four years, any trace of a father's presence being wiped out. It is the child's first reading book, the *Radiant Way* of the title, found in her mother's bookshelf, that brings a few wisps of memory back to the surface, although it takes the information from the family solicitor to reveal the rest of the story.

This is a version of the classic Oedipus story, appropriate for a Freudian analyst: Liz has rejected her mother, and looked to her absent father, but belatedly discovers a crime or the influence of a crime in her father's past. She reconstructs a memory of enjoying reading *The Radiant Way* sitting on her father's knee, and wonders whether her infantile sexuality had laid down feelings of guilt that had somehow been subconsciously associated with her father's disgrace. Liz is in fact relieved – it could have been much worse, she tells Shirley, but she involuntarily reacts with a brief but incapacitating fit of illness in her hotel room, tribute to the ties with the past, which carry such a strong emotional charge.

In spite of the serious concerns with society and individual psychology, the novel has an ironic tone. There is some reflection on the novel-making process, when the narrator cites Jane Austen's famous definition 'Three or four families in a Country Village' as the best subject for a novel: 'A few families in a small, densely populated, parochial, insecure country. Mothers, fathers, aunts, stepchildren, cousins. Where does the story begin and where does it end?' (*RW* 171). On the other hand, the presenting narrator sometimes withholds authoritative assurance, as in the earlier novels. In the description of Brian's and Alix's later state, the narrator's qualifications undermine the whole effect of the positive assurances: they 'are happy. By and large. They have resolved themselves. It seems' (*RW* 164); and later, 'Brian wanted to see socialism in his lifetime. So did Alix. So they said, and they thought they meant it' (*RW* 230–31). Ambiguity of motives and feeling is delicately sketched by leaving its extent to the reader's imagination.

The narrative weaves its different strands together carefully – the important party sequence at the beginning gives way to an account of New Year's Eve in Northam, the Yorkshire town where Liz (and Brian) came from, focusing on Shirley's depressing, dutiful meal for her elderly relatives, and returns to Liz's reflections on her new circumstances and to a long exposition of Alix's situation. Only after this does the narrator insert a characteristic retrospective history of the three main characters, how they met at Cambridge, providing a framework for the anecdotes already given. Their aspirations as young girls are noted – Liz would like to understand, to make sense of things, Alix would like to change things, and Esther would like to acquire interesting information. Only Esther, as she points out, is reasonable in her wishes, and only she, perhaps, can be seen as successful as the text unfolds. The quest to understand and to change things is subject to failures and disappointments, and remains a receding illusion.

Throughout the novel, the interpretation of the past is a vital preliminary to understanding the present, as for instance when Alix muses on her first marriage, blaming herself, as Kate had similarly come to do, but learning a lesson from this:

> She remembered Sebastian, who had been destined to a life of ease. And she with her questions, her doubts, her difficulties, her withdrawals, had destroyed him. Thus she now read the plot of the past. She had not, it seemed, destroyed Nicholas. Not even her great love had destroyed him. She resolved to keep away, to stand out of his light, to let him be. (*RW* 345)

To make sense of the world they live in, then, the characters want to believe that there is a logical cause and effect, that events are not merely random and incomprehensible. In the second novel of the trilogy, this theme is pursued further. The phrase 'natural curiosity' is often used to excuse idle enquiries, but Drabble suggests that the desire to find out, to grasp the reasons for events, is a mainspring in human action, and may even serve as the force to keep human beings alive. Curiosity implies an engagement with life, and Liz fears that losing her sense of curiosity will be a kind of living death: 'Her curiosity is at a low ebb. It occurs to her that not only may she die before she satisfies it, but that she may also lose it before she dies. Curiosity has kept her alive. What if she were to lose it now? She has not the energy to move. She is bored, lifeless' (*NC* 223).

This is however a novel where solutions turn out not to be solutions, but rather demand further investigation, further probing. Even this deeper investigation may not deliver certain results: the reader is left with versions and inventions of the truth suitable to the postmodern world Drabble is depicting. The prime example of this is the family story of Liz Headleand and her sister Shirley; in *The Radiant Way* their unease about their family background had seemed to be solved by the revelation of the probable guilt of their child-molester father, which in turn explained why their punitively severe mother was a recluse. It is, surprisingly, Liz's ex-husband Charles who suggests that there may have been another, earlier trauma in her mother's life which had warped her character even before the disgrace of her husband's arrest.

Again Clive Enderby, the solicitor, produces key documents to explain what had happened in the distant past, and again Liz, as well as Shirley, preoccupied with personal problems and reluctant to discover any further dark secrets, fails to notice the clues and ask the questions that would explain their past. Only at the end, in a party which rivals Liz's opening New Year party in its scope and drama, does the plot suddenly become clear: Liz's mother had been a maid in the house of the aristocratic Percy Hestercombe and had become pregnant by him, the resulting illegitimate child being a daughter now called Marcia Campbell. This, then, is why the Ablewhites had a wine-cooler with the initials of the Hestercombe, Stocklinch and Oxenholme families on the side, initials which have teasingly been shown on Robert Oxenholme's Christmas card, a clue to the fact that a network of family relationships connects Liz's mother's aristocratic seducer to Robert Oxenholme, friend and admirer of Esther Breuer, and also to Henrietta Latchett, Charles Headleand's third wife. This is not however an eighteenth century 'lost heir' plot, and it is neither Liz nor Shirley who is related by blood to these aristocratic lesser characters – only Marcia has this illegitimate blood in her veins, and her half-sisters remain, as they had always been supposed, the children of Alfred and Rita Ablewhite. The significance lies in the new explanations for the way these parents behaved.

The pursuit of explanations into the Ablewhites stops there, but a similar delving into the past is undertaken by Alix on behalf of Paul Whitmore, the murderer who had been captured in the flat above Esther's that evening when Liz and Alix had been visiting Esther. *The Radiant Way* had focused on the murders and their victims. *A Natural Curiosity* however traces a quest to find out why Paul Whitmore became a murderer. The novel opens with Alix driving across the moors to visit him, now imprisoned fairly close to her present home in Northam. As she drives through the mist, she has 'the illusion of moving in a small patch of light, her own pocket of clarity' (NC 2), a neat image for the limited subjective interpretations that are imposed by Alix and by other characters on the flow of the past. Paul Whitmore finally succeeds in getting Alix to find out the attitude of his mother, which eventually she manages to do. Angela Malkin, as his mother now calls herself, is a strange and evil woman, who keeps a kennel for large dogs; after a first hostile encounter, Alix is reluctant to visit her again, but on a second, more violent and gruesome confrontation discovers that Angela has been starving a large enclosure of dogs to death.

For Alix, who has been unwilling to believe in motiveless malignancy in her murderer, these are all in a way satisfactory discoveries: 'He had been mothered by a mad woman, a fury, a harpy, a gorgon. He had been tormented, like the dogs, in a punishment block, with bloody treats hanging out of reach over his head. Poor Paul was exonerated. Angela is the guilty one. The finger points at Angela' (NC 287). Yet, behind these mysteries, further chains of cause and effect lead into the past. Why had Angela become the destructive harpy presented here? We find that Paul had been a twin, and his baby twin sister had died, a shock which may have twisted Angela's personality, causing her to blame Paul and ill-treat him throughout his childhood. But then why was she mentally fragile enough to give way under this tragedy? The answers can be eternally deferred, will be lost in the mists of time. Similarly one might ask why Rita Ablewhite was seduced by Percy Hestercombe, when other maids were not, and why she ended up marrying the inadequate Alfred Ablewhite.

Liz's and Alix's interest in human nature both coincide and diverge here – Alix suggests that Paul Whitmore is 'a kind of living experiment ... we can learn from him if we can learn how to' (NC 62), while Liz, as a psychiatrist, takes a different view. As in her earliest student days, her desire is still to understand things: 'What I do suffer from is curiosity. I want to know what really happened', she tells her friend Ivan Warner – 'At the beginning. When human nature began. At the beginning of human time. And I know I'll never know. But I can't stop looking' (NC 75). Liz is driven to ask whether the nature of humanity is implicitly flawed: 'That something went wrong at the beginning of human nature, of human nurture, that humanity mistook itself fatally, for ever?' (NC 24).

The brief final scene reunites Liz, Alix and Esther, as the conclusion of *The Radiant Way* had done, this time in Italy, and it is here that doubt is cast on the ability of curiosity ever to find the answers it seeks. Liz has looked forward to finding the complete truth about human nature, but more realistically she has mental reservations about Alix's explanation of Paul Whitmore's murderousness; she reflects that 'Paul's father is a perfectly normal, indeed quite kind-hearted chap, and that many children grow up fairly normal without any parental kindness at all. At least they do not grow up into mass murderers'(NC 302). Alix is herself surprised that Paul 'should have turned out to fit so neatly the sort of explanation that I might be expected to find for him', but Esther points out that in a way Alix has selected the puzzle for herself, as this is the kind of murderer (a vegetarian, interested in Ancient History) that she would naturally take an interest in. 'So I haven't proved anything,' Alix concludes, 'I've just confirmed my own pre-judices about human nature' (NC 302).

Almost equally impenetrable are the reasons for the broad social movements which in turn clearly affect the characters. The eighties, identified with the Conservative Thatcher government, were, as mentioned already, encouraging enterprise and entrepreneurial activities, and leaving weaker businesses to fail, without assistance or compensation. In this novel, the pressure has been taken off Brian and Alix after their move to Northam, where a socialist local government system is still promoting some social programmes, but Shirley, Liz's sister, and her husband Cliff Harper exemplify the harshness of the new regime towards small businesses. Cliff and his partner run a small factory making car wing mirrors and small picnic sets, a business that comes under economic pressure, and he is glimpsed at intervals throughout the novel becoming more and more confused, strained and tense, until he commits suicide.

The death of Cliff, the introduction of an unknown half-sister for Liz, and the revelation that Paul Whitmore's mother was spectacularly abusing the dogs in her charge are all startling plot developments – these events interlock with the other pieces of the plot, supplying missing motives or culminating in a series of forces. Yet the plotting of this novel with its large cast of characters has a strangely random effect. Alix's encounter with Angela Malkin is juxtaposed with Liz's television appearance talking about child sex and death, Cliff's suicide and Shirley's subsequent impulsive flight. Some hypotheses about the causes of these developments, however, like the suggestions about Angela Malkin's motives, may seem insecure and ultimately unprovable, yet many developments of the plot are finally tied down to at least immediate plausible origins, and this is extended to the assumption that beneath all life events is a framework of cause and effect, especially heredity, as Liz muses to herself:

> The force of repetition is terrible, terrible. We assemble strangers at random gatherings, we shake off parents and lovers and husbands and wives and children. We miscegenate and emigrate, we fly to the uttermost parts of the earth, and yet the same face grins at us, the same hand beckons us. There is no escape.
> And is that all there is to it? *All?* (*NC* 249)

The organizing narrator emphasizes that episodes are being selected and invented to illustrate specific points, even points about ambiguity, and addresses the reader to emphasize the partial, skewed picture of human relationships which is being given in this narrative:

> it has to be said that none of the Headland children will get much of an appearance here. They will serve only as occasional chorus. There are too many of them to be treated individually. And anyway, Charles himself is only a small subplot. This is not the Headland saga. You do not have to retain these names, these relationships. (*NC* 30)

The characters both are and are not real – the organizing narrator describes Robert Holland, the man who takes Shirley to Paris when she runs away from home after Cliff's suicide, as a construction: 'I have made him as plausible as I can, I have offered him motivation, but I have to admit that it doesn't seem probable that he and Shirley can continue to go on seeing one another' (*NC* 254), whereas Shirley herself is endowed with an independent will, and for her the presenting narrator explains: 'Many endings have occurred to Shirley, more, perhaps than have occurred to you or me ... None of these endings seem very plausible, very likely. But then Shirley's behaviour for the past months has been highly unlikely. It astonished me, it astonished her, and maybe it astonished you'. As in *The Realms of Gold*, the narrator challenges the reader:[4] 'What do *you* think will happen to her? Do *you* think our end is known in our beginning, that we are predetermined, that we endlessly repeat?' (*NC* 251–2).

The title of the third part of the trilogy refers to one of the two gates through which dreams were said to be sent to sleepers, as described in the prologue extract from *The Odyssey*: 'the dreams that come to us through the traitor ivory deceive us with false images of what will never come to pass'. Many dreams attract the characters in this novel, but the main plot line involves Stephen Cox, friend of Brian and Alix Bowen and of Liz Headleand: he aims to visit Cambodia (then Kampuchea) to gather material for a play about the dictator Pol Pot. Behind this project lies Stephen's fascination with the proclaimed programme of Pol Pot and his Khmer Rouge army, that of returning the country to the stone age, shaking off western and other corruption, and starting a new, just society from scratch. The extreme bloodshed involved in wiping out all traces of corrupt civilization does not deter Stephen from tracing an ideal of innocence and fairness which is nowhere to be found in the rest of the world. Is a return to primal simplicity possible? He recalls using the words 'fatal curiosity' to Liz, and indeed his dream leads him to his death.

On another level, Stephen's quest for material about Pol Pot evokes the theme of ambiguity and uncertainty: it is, like many of those in *A Natural Curiosity*, doomed to failure, as nobody has certain facts about the dictator's life, or even his true name.

The narrator begins the novel with the statement that 'This is a novel – if novel it be – about Good Time and Bad Time' (*GI* 3). Good time is roughly identified with the material wealth and consumer goods of western society – the materialism that Pol Pot rejects – and includes all luxuries of whatever origin; Bad Time comprises extreme poverty, starvation, sickness, individual misfortune and also war, revolution, oppression and its atrocities.

> Good Time and Bad Time coexist. We in Good Time receive messengers who stumble across the bridge or through the river, maimed and bleeding, shocked and starving. They try to tell us what it is like over there, and we try to listen.

But the narrator adds 'Some step into Bad Time suddenly. It may be waiting there, in the next room' (*GI* 3–4) – and Bad Time is later used to refer to personal disaster. Brian Bowen becomes very ill, off-stage and in a muted facet of the plot. 'Brian is entering Bad Time', the narrator tells us, and though he has a successful operation and recovers, Alix has been overwhelmed by the helplessness and degradation experienced by the sick:

> She had hated the indignity, the reductiveness of sickness ... the shabby ward, the communal lavatory, the colourless drained old men with stubble beards, the plastic bed curtains, the walking drips, the smells, the institutional cooking, the pert bossy little nurses ... The shadow has fallen but she will ignore it, and look the other way, into the light. She will forget that premature insight into decline, helplessness, dependence, bedpans, and, worst of all, the indifferent contempt of the healthy young. (*GI* 433)

This kind of Bad Time directly threatens even Good Time westerners, and in spite of Alix's feeling that money could cushion the sick person from these evils, decline and helplessness are not, ultimately, escapable.

The theme of the novel, however, is related mainly to the interpretation of Bad Time as Good Time by Stephen and a few others. A near parody of Stephen's wistful idealism is presented in Akira, the Japanese photographer, who is obsessed by the Khmer Rouge programme:

> A small nation, a few million people with nothing but their own bare hands. No rockets, no aeroplanes, no tanks. They wished to remake mankind in a new image. Who can say they did not mean well? They were poisoned by their enemies and by their friends. Americans, Russians, all guilty. They wished to be self-sufficient. They wished to detach themselves from the wheel of wickedness that is the world. Who can deny them that right? That hope? (*GI* 230)

This echoes the dreams of a fairer society voiced in the earlier novels, for instance by Alix, influenced by her public-spirited boarding school, or by Brian, an unreconstructed socialist, but here it is writ large as whole nations struggle in different ways with Bad Time. Stephen himself has lost most of his deceptive dream before he gets to Cambodia, and Akira only prolongs the deception:

A breath of hope stirs like a sweet corrupt poison in his entrails. It is as though Akira were telling him that God, after all, is not dead, and salvation is still on offer. History is reprieved, the dead did not die in vain, the dry bones will live.

The immensity of this utterly impossible hope reveals to him the immensity of his depression, of his prolonged mourning for the death of the dream. So, he had, once, after all, hoped. He had, once, after all, believed that the future would be better, better *in kind*, than the past.

... Stephen believes no longer, but he wants Akira to believe. He wants Akira to be damned on his behalf, and on behalf of Malcolm Caldwell, and Brian Bowen and Perry Blinkhorn, and all those who were inched towards the loss of faith. He wants Akira to prove the possibility of damnation or salvation. (*GI* 228–30)

Stephen, then, has departed a few years before *The Gates of Ivory* opens, at a point depicted in *A Natural Curiosity*, and investigation of his journey begins with Liz receiving a motley parcel from Cambodia containing assorted papers and photographs, and, most intriguingly, two finger-bones (Stephen had been given them as a good luck charm, it seems). An isolated figure, Stephen has cut himself off from his own family, and has put Liz down on his passport as next of kin.

In Thailand Stephen meets Miss Porntip, a fascinating ex-beauty queen, now a very successful business woman, who is attracted to him and tries to convince him that the Good Time of spreading capitalism is much better than the misery of primitive poverty: ' "Is better now," she tells Stephen. "Is better life expectancy, more electrics, more saloon cars, more soap, more rice, more nice clothings and suitings, more ice-cream, more maple syrup, more Coca-Cola ..." ' (*GI* 106). But Stephen is not convinced.

The photographs in Liz's parcel were taken by Konstantin Vassiliou, a character seen as a small boy in *The Needle's Eye*, eldest son of Rose Vassiliou, now a prize-winning photographer (and inheritor of his grandfather's wealth). Konstantin is an attractive young man, who believes he bears a charmed life, and sympathizes with Stephen's quest: 'Konstantin is Stephen's good angel. Miss Porntip is his bad angel' (*GI* 99), the narrator tells us, perhaps not altogether reliably. He travels with Stephen and Akira into the interior of Cambodia, where they are eventually seized by a group of Khmer soldiers. Akira is led away into the forest and never seen again; Stephen and Konstantin are left in a remote village, where Stephen becomes desperately ill. Eventually Konstantin, believing Stephen to be dying, leaves alone, and we last see Stephen, slightly better, being taken on to a Cambodian clinic of poor reputation. It is only when Liz heroically follows his trail as far as Hanoi that she meets with news of Stephen's death, delivered by that recurrent character in Drabble's novels, Gabriel Denham, who happens to be filming in Cambodia.

The novel includes several references to the novels of Conrad, especially *Victory*, set in the countries where Stephen travels, and when Liz reads *Victory*, in an attempt to broaden her background knowledge of the area, she reacts with hostility to its narrative method:

> What is the point of all this skipping about from one time scale to another? Is it incompetence or ingenuity? And if it is ingenuity, what is Conrad being ingenious about? Liz likes to know where she is in a novel. She likes a novel that begins at the beginning and moves inexorably to its end. She does not like confusion for its own sake. There is plenty of confusion in real life, without inventing more of it. (*GI* 238)

This joke reminds the reader that *The Gates of Ivory* has a complex dual time-scheme, moving to and fro between Stephen's actual experiences, two years earlier, and his friends' erratic attempts to piece together what has become of him, amid the onward pressure of their own diverse lives. This also has the effect of dividing the narrative again into observed and observer sections, as in *A Summer Bird-Cage*, *The Waterfall* and *The Needle's Eye*; Stephen's pilgrimage is contrasted with the busy urban lives of his friends, though this is mainly perceived by the reader, through the presentation of the narrator, while his friends gain only wisps and rumours of his progress through indirect sources.

A further narrative ingenuity lies in the introduction of some sections of first-person narrative by Hattie Osborne, a character new to the trilogy; she is a very beautiful ex-actress who was discovered as a girl at a Butlins holiday camp – by who else but Gabriel Denham – and after a few roles in minor films has become a not very successful literary and theatrical agent of a kind. Now about 40 years old, Hattie has moved in theatrical circles for many years and, though claiming to be ignorant and uneducated, scatters a range of literary allusions and quotations through her account of her friendship with Stephen. In a surprising plot development she and Aaron Headland, Liz's middle stepson, fall in love, and she becomes pregnant, the birth of her baby coinciding with Stephen's memorial service and the end of the novel; the path to Stephen's death recommences with the creation of new life. Her first-person narrative introduces a jokey, edgy tone to the novel, as she exaggerates the detachment of the usual Drabble narrator, and criticizes the other characters, including Liz and Alix, from an external point of view, contrasting with the third-person narrator's omniscient approach, which gives the thoughts of most characters and by explaining their motives tends to be more sympathetic.

Parallel to Stephen's quest for the kernel of radical social change is the quest of a Vietnamese woman, Mme Savet Akrun, who has lost her son Mitra in the course of her family's refugee wanderings. Konstantin's photograph of her, captioned 'Where is my son?' has been used on a charity poster, and her plight, as she is visited in turn by Konstantin, Stephen and Liz, emblematizes the Bad Time inflicted by war and ideology, which visitors from the Good Time can only sympathize with but not reverse. As yet another parallel strand, Rose Vassiliou fears that her son too is lost for ever, because no communication has been received from Konstantin since the fatal expedition into the forest of Cambodia, but this loss has a happier outcome: news of Stephen's memorial service reaches Konstantin and breaks the two years' silence of guilt and shame at his responsibility (as he sees it) for abandoning Stephen to his death: a dramatic reunion with the patient Rose in the middle of the memorial service balances the loss of the dream with the saving of the individual.

Stephen's dream of finding the germ of a just society has faded away during his final illness. As he lies waiting for death, he rejects the idea of a heavenly insight in his last moments: 'It was not very interesting, there would be no revelation, no confrontation, no lights from Heaven would flash, neither God nor Pol Pot would speak from the burning bush. There would be no message to take back to the shores of the living' (*GI* 355).

The memorial service equally emphasizes that there is no answer to his doubts and dreams. Alix weeps at the appropriate opening hymn, as the congregation sing:

> Would man but wake from out his haunted sleep,
> Earth might be fair, and all men glad and wise.

> <div align="right">(<i>GI</i> 438)</div>

Alix asks:

> Why *could* not man wake from his haunted sleep? Why must it go on for ever and ever, death and destruction, tragic empire after tragic empire ... Will the killing ever stop, will the Numbers Game ever be played out, will atrocities ever cease, will the choir and the congregation be able to rise to the crescendo? No, of course not. (*GI* 438–9)

The answer to the dream is a negative one: 'when I became a woman, I put away childish things, thinks Alix: things such as hymns, prayers, God, hope' (*GI* 439). The organizing narrator, as in other novels, insists on the malleability of the plot material:

> This story could have been the story of the search for and the discovery of Mme Akrun's son Mitra: a moving human-interest story, with a happy ending, a reunion ending, with music. Or it could have been the story of the search for and discovery of Stephen Cox ... Such a narrative would have required a certain amount of trickiness, a certain deployment of not-quite-acceptable coincidences, a certain ruthless tidying up of the random movements of people and peoples. But it should not be beyond the competence of a certain kind of reasonably experienced novelist. One may force, one may impose one's will.
>
> But such a narrative will not do. The mismatch between narrative and subject is too great. Why impose the story line of individual fate upon a story which is at least in part to do with numbers? A queasiness, a moral scruple overcomes the writer at the prospect of selecting individuals from the mass of history, from the human soup. Why this one, why not another? Why pause here? Why discriminate? Why seek the comfort of the particular, the anguish of the particular? (*GI* 137–8)

The narrative has perhaps sentimentally kept Konstantin Vassiliou alive to return to his mother, but Mitra Akrun must remain lost, to stand for the millions of others who are not saved. It is not possible to tell the story of everybody, and the multiple plot strands of this novel can only try to illustrate the varying possibilities, in the same way that the mocking lists of the possible fates of Mitra Akrun in fact show the many fates of his contemporaries:

> Mitra pushes a glittering articulated snake of super-trolleys down a gleaming corridor in Toronto, whistling as he goes.
> Mitra bends over his medical text books in an attic in a Parisian suburb and late into the night he studies the names of the small bones and the large.
> Mitra lies in a field hospital of delicate bamboo, delirious, with a newly amputated leg.
> Mitra in a smart pastiche uniform of white and gold and green bows low at the gateway to the Shangri-La hotel... (*GI* 159)

So Mme Akrun does not find her son, but Rose Vassiliou finds hers; Stephen dies, but Brian Bowen recovers.

Stephen's memorial service, organized by Liz and Alix, concludes the trilogy, the memorial reception at Liz's house balancing the huge party at the Headleands' Harley Street house with which the sequence began. The previous two volumes however had both ended with the three friends Liz, Alix and Esther united on a quiet holiday; to incorporate this motif as well as the concluding party, Drabble inserts a flash forward to a sunny Yorkshire walking tour. It is with the two sons however that the last pages are concerned: Rose and Konstantin Vassiliou are reunited, but they, the narrator tells us, 'belong to a different world and a different density. They have wandered into the story from the old-fashioned, Freudian, psychological novel, and they cannot mix and mingle with the guests of Liz Headleand. They should never have been invited' (*GI* 461).

Mitra Akrun is transformed in the last paragraph of the book into a guerrilla soldier, determined to fight for his own dream. 'He is multitudes' (*GI* 462); he represents the multitudes that cannot be included in one novel, the multitudes that the reader is invited to remember.

8

Mothers and Others

The next two novels take a less pleasantly ironic tone than the previous trilogy: although the plots do not include as much horrific material as the mass killings of *The Gates of Ivory*, the narrator shows little indulgence towards any of the individual characters. The tone is detached and critical, and even pleasant descriptions, such as of the country house where the first scene opens, are qualified by negative aspects: the roses in the rose garden have a 'rotting, fecal, fungal smell' (*WE* 17), the little tender tendrils of the virginia creeper round the window embower a dead bird. Patsy, the owner of the house, is condemned for denying problems in her own family: 'That's a bit harsh, but why not be harsh?' (*WE* 121) the narrator adds robustly.

Margaret Drabble says that she was concerned that the reader should not be allowed to identify with any of the characters; the novel was conceived as a satire on bourgeois selfishness, and she did not wish their behaviour to be seen with sympathy.[1] While trying to finish *The Gates of Ivory* she had said

> If ever I finish it ... perhaps I will then retreat and write a pastoral novel with a small cast of thoroughly English characters, set in a small village – a novel accepting the geographical limitations of Mrs Gaskell's *Cranford*, of Jane Austen's *Emma*.[2]

In fact the novel illustrates what she had foreseen, 'the near-impossibility of writing peaceful regional traditional rural fiction in a poisoned landscape of undrinkable water, over-fertilized soil, dangerous nuclear plants, and brain-mad cows'.[3]

Thematically, the novel returns to Stephen's concern for the just society. Denied in *The Gates of Ivory*, the dream is attacked again in *The Witch of Exmoor*, but where the former novel glanced at the distorted and decayed attempts of the Khmer people to bring the dream into being, the latter keeps this ideal as a theoretical hypothesis, toyed with by the characters.

This theme determines the opening scene of the novel which depicts, not the Witch of Exmoor of the title, otherwise known as Frieda Haxby, but her three grown-up children (Daniel, Gogo and Rosemary), their spouses and children. As they chat, Gogo's husband David D'Anger propounds his favourite social game, the Veil of Ignorance,[4] which asks players to work out some fundamental principles of social justice, whereby they might accept existence in such a society, even if they were disabled, poor or otherwise disadvantaged. As a talking point, this game recurs during the narrative, a token of the problems of an unjust society as it exists in Britain. Drabble says that she would have liked more critical attention paid to this idea, which is one which particularly interests her.[5] David D'Anger is a Guyanese of Indian descent, and a parliamentary candidate, later a Member of Parliament. He is also an idealist, and the presenting narrator, moving then into authoritative narration, challenges the reader simultaneously to accept his plausibility and to acknowledge the justice of his point of view:

> Is this possible, you ask, in the late twentieth century? We concede it was possible for men and women to create, even to believe in such images in the past – as late as the nineteenth century these possibilities lingered – but surely we know better now? We are adult now, and have put away childish things ... Imagine David D'Anger. You say he is an impossibility, and you cannot imagine him, any more than he can imagine the nature of the revolution that would bring about the world he thinks he wishes to construct. But you are wrong. The truth is that you, for David D'Anger, are the impossibility. The present world which we seem to inhabit is an impossibility. He cannot live at ease in it, he cannot believe it is real. (*WE* 47)

The family is a prosperous one – Daniel and Patsy Palmer work as barrister and censorship executive respectively, while Gogo is a neurologist; the youngest sibling Rosemary works in the media and her husband Nathan Herz is in advertising. All are therefore well paid, and only Nathan, who is otherwise fairly unscrupulous in his profession, says he would be willing to risk moving to a just society where he might lose his comforts and privileges.

Occasionally seen as a contrast to this middle-class cast of characters, Will Paine is a young half-Jamaican man, victim of a heavy prison sentence for selling marijuana, to whom Patsy has offered accommodation and pocket money for doing odd jobs around the house. Will is a sweet-natured person who manages to feel that he has been lucky in life, in spite of his obvious disadvantages. He compares his lot to that of refugees and victims of war and famine in the third world, and feels that even an ex-convict in Britain has much to be thankful for. His precarious existence, however – for Patsy finds his presence burdensome after a while and ejects him without finding him a suitable place to go to – is a reminder of the struggles of the less fortunate in the unjust society.

Frieda Haxby too, though highly successful in her career as a historian, indeed more successful and celebrated than any of her children, is now divesting herself of material goods; she sells the house in Romley where the family was brought up, and buys a huge derelict ex-hotel on the very brink of the North Devon coast. Possession of a mansion, however dilapidated, is a far cry from poverty or dependency, but Frieda does not make any attempt to renovate her decaying abode, and camps there as if a refugee in alien territory. Because of this rejection of material comfort, and partly because of her unwillingness to see them, her children consider that she is going mad. The first half of the novel is concerned with their attempts to persuade her to behave more normally, and Frieda's own pursuit of her reclusive way of life.

There is thus a repetition of Drabble's recurrent family drama here, of the hostile sisters and the tyrannical mother encountered in earlier novels, but in this case the younger generation is a pale shadow of the pattern buried in Frieda's past. She herself is not a burdensome, repressive mother, in spite of the anxiety she causes her children: as an abandoned wife, a hard worker supporting her family, she has not had time to oppress her children, and now in her sixties she 'has forced them into the role of Bad Children, and wilfully, playfully, cast herself as a Neglected Mother' (WE 86). But Frieda's own mother has been a domestic tyrant, an unloving parent, and later Frieda and her elder sister Everhilda had been locked into a hostile triangle with Frieda's husband, Everhilda's lover, Andrew Palmer. Frieda believes that Everhilda tried to kill her as a child, as she climbed up a ladder in an old mill, and knows more certainly that Everhilda and Andrew had been lovers (continuously or 'on-and-off'?) throughout her own married life. Those last weeks of her marriage seem to have culminated in Frieda's learning the truth, and Everhilda committing suicide, also killing, like Stephen in *The Realms of Gold*, her illegitimate baby daughter.

All this is embedded in Frieda's memoirs, which she has typed into her computer, where it is found by her granddaughter Emily. The story seems to explain Frieda's cynical and detached attitude towards her family and society's expectations in general, and the character of Frieda, intermittently revealed in short sections depicting her life on Exmoor, is an interesting one. However, Frieda disappears from the narrative about halfway through, and the focus shifts to her children's efforts to find out what has become of her, and to the contents of her will.

Paradoxically it is Will Paine who is the last person to see Frieda alive; he drifts across southern England, looking for likely contacts and refuges, and manages to extract some shelter and odd jobs from Frieda on the grounds that he knew her grandchildren. She, like Patsy, ejects him after a while, but bestows on him large amounts of money from an illegal American bank account, enough to take him to Jamaica and beyond. Frieda's body is washed up further down the coast a month later, and it seems at that point unclear whether she fell while on one of her mussel-gathering walks, or deliberately drowned herself, due to fear of fatal illness.

Throughout the narrative, the concern of Frieda's children has been motivated largely by greed; the presenting narrator remains detached and does not endorse or contradict the reader's assumed reactions:

> They have little excuse for what you may take to be their greed and selfishness... But you have not reckoned with two important considerations. The first of these is family jealousy, that long-ago, ancient, fairytale hatred which means that a brother does not like his sisters to gain at his expense – particularly when those sisters are not themselves in need. The second is the more immediate legacy of the last twenty years. Greed and selfishness have become respectable. Like family jealousy, they are not new, but they have gained a new sanction. It is now considered correct to covet. (*WE* 120)

Frieda is one of the few people to express criticism of society: she points to the unsafe and cruel workings of the food industry, and the pressure of business on products that everyone uses. Poor observation of public safety has also led to the sinking of a pleasure steamer on the Thames, where many young people, including an office worker, Belle, from Nathan's advertising company, were drowned in the middle of a party. Belle had been a joyous, beautiful, spontaneous young girl, and although she had rejected his advances because she was a lesbian, Nathan had continued to love her. This incident is based on a real event, the sinking of *The Marchioness*, and Margaret Drabble mentions that in her view an additional appalling factor of the loss of *The Marchioness* was the attitude of the public who considered that the deaths of a lot of young people who were having a party was not of any consequence, might even be said to serve them right.[6]

As the others had feared, Frieda's will leaves all she has to Gogo's and David's son Benjie. Even worse, a slightly earlier will, which might have a slight chance of being preferred, leaves twenty thousand pounds each to her children, but all the residue in trust to David D'Anger for the purpose of establishing 'the Just Society' in the Valley of the Eagles in Guyana. The whole family is horrified by both the inequitable testaments, and Benjie, an exceptionally intelligent and alert child, begins to sink into feverish depression, this new selection as 'special' only reinforcing his parents' excessive expectations of him. As a friend of David remarks, 'it's one hell of an old fashioned plot. Wills, legacies, inheritance tax, capital gains tax. A real old nineteenth-century property plot' (*WE* 215).

Here, then, the theme of the just society reappears. David and Frieda had discussed the idea, particularly of an experimental just society set up as a closed system, protected from the pressures of trade, immigration, international currency changes, agreements and other external forces. This ghost of Pol Pot's Cambodian experiment reappears in a vision of a small-scale trial in Guyana, and David feels guilty about influencing Frieda to take such an interest in his theories. Like several other Drabble characters before him, most notably the ambivalent Stephen Cox, David shrinks before the impossibility of changing expectations and behaviour enough to redirect society on an entirely new course. 'David D'Anger knows that the Just Society is an impossibility ... but he does not like to know that he knows it' (WE 205).

His in-laws are evidence of this, in their self-centred complacency. A series of crises afflicts them, linked to their weaknesses and perhaps interpretable as punishments: Nathan, the most personally generous though devoid of social scruples, dies of a heart attack, while Rosemary develops kidney failure. Daniel's and Patsy's son Simon, whose descent into drugged ineffectiveness they have ignored, dies walking along a motorway. David and Gogo are undermined and their confidence weakened by Benjie's illness. Out of these traumas some hope emerges, suggesting a mitigation of the narrative's condemnation of the human race: Emily and Benjie are still idealistic.

As often appears in Drabble's novels, then, some members of the younger generation seem to have escaped from the hereditary or environmental doom that afflicted their elders. Benjie's escape is precarious, in that his grandmother's legacy, and his parents' excessive expectations have led to his almost sinking under their pressure, affectionate and generous though it is compared with the pressure exerted by monster parents of earlier novels. In keeping with the motif of inheritance, Frieda sees her own ambition as 'her mother's, inherited, transferred, a deadly legacy' (WE 135). Simon conversely suffered from his parents' neglect, compounded by the neglect of his university tutor.

As appropriate for a novel with a character named Gogo, some of the passages of comment chime with the nihilism of *Waiting for Godot*. Frieda's musings could have been spoken by Beckett's Gogo and Didi:

> The personal decays from us, leaving us with no memory of it, although we know that it has been. But it was at its strongest nothing more than an evolutionary trick, a spasm of self gripping to a wet rock. We were born without meaning, we struggled without meaning, we met and married and loved and hated without meaning. We are accidents. All our passions are arbitrary, trivial, a game of hazard, like this game of patience which I now play. (WE 136)

Nonetheless, the narrator is careful to pin this free indirect speech down to Frieda's own point of view in the last sentence; it is not the authoritative voice of the narrator. Her children

Gogo and Rosemary, whose new sisterly affection at the end of the novel is another of the limited, happier results of the harsh plot events, return to the issues of heredity and upbringing, trying to find sense, cause and effect: 'They piece together their fears of the past and for the future, and each time they meet a new pattern emerges, a new seam is stitched. One day they will make sense of their ancestry. Are they unique, are they freaks, are they throw-backs, are they pioneers of a new order? Frieda had left them with so many questions unanswered' (WE 267).

Interpretation is as usual uncertain, as other Drabble characters have found: Frieda writes her memoirs both as revenge and to raise the dead, to impose her view and judgement on the past, as well as to find out what it was. As she says, 'There were so many versions of the story, and all of them were false... you could tell the story any old way, as long as you left out most of the circumstantial details' (WE 113–15).

The narrator seems in fact to tease the reader by offering an opportunity to guess the story, before revealing the 'truth' within the narrative, and telling the reader 'You have not guessed quite right about Nathan...' (WE 17) and, as noted above, 'You say [David D'Anger] is an impossibility ... you are wrong' (WE 47). There is a curious insistence on using 'We':

> Now we may return to Lily McNab. You remember the name of Lily McNab, child psychotherapist? We have not yet been introduced. We have several possibilities with Ms McNab. Is she a scholarly grey-haired owl-spectacled Scot with an Edinburgh accent? An imported American from New York? A Belsize Park matron ...? We had better take care ...' (WE 230)

The reader is also addressed as 'you', a practice some find coercive, but it can be a joke, as the presenting narrator implies by a quick change of pronouns in the discussion of the D'Angers' habit of surveying ethnic minorities: 'You might think this indicates an unhealthy obsession with racial origins, and you might be right. On the other hand, you might put it down to a natural sociological curiosity. I don't have to have a view on this, I am simply reporting the facts' (WE 98).

Margaret Drabble wrote a fantasy postscript for the novel, which was excised from the British edition but appears in the American edition. In it, the dead Frieda, Nathan and Belle (the girl who drowned on the pleasure boat) are in heaven, which takes the form of a beautiful, well serviced cruise boat, perhaps because they all died in or near the water. They discuss the past, and Frieda reveals that her death had been an accident. Also, she had meant well in leaving her money to Benjie, had hoped to give him some scope to make something of his life, and is much dismayed to find she had miscalculated. Her benevolent intentions are however asserted, possibly reminding us that good qualities have after all existed in her, as in Nathan and Belle, and that human nature is not universally bad. Paradoxically the hope for the future is distributed between the young, as yet untried, Emily and Benjie, and the now dead Belle, Nathan and Frieda.

After *The Witch of Exmoor*'s rather different version of the mother problem, Margaret Drabble moved to the hybrid genre of fictionalized semi-biography of her own mother, Marie Drabble, born Kathleen Marie Bloor. This is a three-generation story of which the account of the eldest generation follows as closely as possible what Drabble knows about her parents. Her mother's fictional counterpart is called Bessie Bawtry, her father becomes Joe Barron, and again a major theme is that of heredity. Once more, the narrative asks whether individual destiny is possible, given the straitjacket of heredity, reinforced by the pattern of upbringing and environment which equally restricts the individual. The approach of the novel to this theme verges on the tragic, as heredity affects the characters like a curse, which they try to evade, with little success, at least for the older generation. 'Escape' is a key word, as the characters struggle in the grip of their genetic heritage, and, according to the narrator, can only cheat the destiny laid down for them by unexpected mutations altering their personalities, or by chance collisions with new conditions or people.

Yet at first Bessie and Joe, and some of their relations, seem to break away from their genetic heritage: Bessie is the ambitious but fragile daughter of a working-class couple; her keen intelligence and hard work win her a scholarship to Cambridge, but she is unable to make a further leap to escape into the wider world. Her childhood sweetheart Joe Barron, son of the owner of a small glassware factory, fails to win a scholarship, but eventually persuades his family to support him at Cambridge, where he renews friendship with Bessie.

100

After graduating, instead of striking out into a brave new world, both return to their home town – Joe as a barrister, Bessie as a school teacher – where they later marry. Their marriage becomes one of endurance, as Bessie deteriorates into a depressive complainer who blames her husband and children for her dissatisfaction, and inflicts on them her irrational demands and explosive bad temper.

Why did Bessie Bawtry fail to make her own way in the world; why did she return 'with her tail between her legs?' (*PM* 128). The narrator suggests various reasons – a loss of nerve, a recurrent pattern of giving way to illness as an evasion of effort, failure at interviews because of her Yorkshire accent – without finding any of them satisfactory.

Asking whether Joe marries Bessie out of pity, or love, the narrator points out that 'We would not be asking these questions had all turned out well for Joe and Bessie. But all did not turn out well. We do not know the details of what went wrong' (*PM* 131). The narrator even prays, passionately, for the story to be changed, for the past to be annihilated: 'Where is Joe Barron, all this while? Please God that he has escaped too. If he has escaped Bessie, then all can be undone. Let it be undone. Let it all never have happened. Let it be unwound, unstitched, unwounded' (*PM* 115). She wishes for Bessie to change, to defy genetic encoding by mutating, to become more independent and successful as an individual, as this would release Joe, even if it meant that their children would never exist: 'Not to be born is best, as the ancients said. Can't somebody tell that, now, to Bessie Bawtry and Joe Barron, before they inflict their short-comings and their misgivings and their indecisions upon their suffering gene pool and bloodline? Can't somebody warn them before it is too late?' (*PM* 115).

As the title indicates, then, this is a novel which suggests that the effects of heredity and environment together are a pressure that few can evade. The peppered moth, which in its Latin name, *Biston betularia*, shares its initials with Bessie Bawtry, is a moth which in the south of England is light coloured, and in the northern industrial areas is dark, because the light moths are unable to camouflage themselves against the uniformly sooty surfaces of the north, and are picked off by predators, leaving only fortuitously dark siblings to perpetuate their dark genes. A moth is unable to change its spots by will-power alone, and so the efforts of the characters in this novel are unlikely to succeed without aid. The entomological imagery is unflattering to Bessie, who is presented as 'like a white worm' (*PM* 225), 'some chrysalis, some meaningless waxy body container, in which a new form of life was trying to hatch' (*PM* 98).

The tragic tone of the narrative deepens, as young Bessie's enjoyment of Cambridge drama, including Greek tragedies *The Bacchae* and *Elektra*, is described, followed immediately by a discussion of evolution, where the narrator raises the possibility of Bessie's mutation. Bessie, however, has only partially mutated – she has used her brains vigorously to enter a new kind of life, but, the narrative seems to suggest, she has not mutated enough to conquer and live in a different environment. 'If Bessie mutates now,' says the narrator, 'then Joe will be saved and all that may come to be will be cancelled, and posterity will be spared' (*PM* 115); but Bessie does not mutate, and she fulfils what her genes have shaped her to become.

As Drabble explains in the Afterword, she has excluded her real life sisters and brother, and her own three children, from the novel, giving Bessie and Joe instead two children, Robert and Chrissie, and one grandchild, Chrissie's daughter Faro. In these fictional generations, the pattern of heredity is gradually altered, and possibilities open up. The novel begins in the present time, with a public meeting about a project to take and analyse the mitochondrial DNA of women in Breaseborough (a fictional small town based on Mexborough, Drabble's grand-parents' home town). This DNA would be compared with that of a stone-age man recently discovered in the neighbourhood, thus producing some evidence about the continuance of the same families in this locality in South Yorkshire. Against the back-ground of interest in heredity, the inheritance of the characters from their parents and grandparents is played out, and the possibility of individual destiny breaking away from this is resurrected.

So we see Chrissie, Bessie's daughter, trying to be different from her parents, but in fact following the same pattern under a few superficial changes:

> She went to an ancient university because that's what she was programmed to do. She didn't yet know it, but she was programmed

to follow in her parents' footsteps. Most people are. It takes a lot of effort to break the pattern. It costs a lot. A hundred pages back Chrissie's future, like her past, had been utterly unformulated. Anything had been possible. But the nearer she got to the future, the more her past filled in with inherited and acquired characteristics, and the further that freedom fled. (*PM* 213)

At this point the organizing narrator makes a link between the process of story-making and the unfolding of a life, where the choices seem open but in fact are constrained by the environment and mindset of the individual:

The story could, in theory, have gone in many different directions. But in practice the options are as limited as they are in computerized, apparently open-ended works of interactive fiction. The imagination fails to supply the necessary freedom. It loops back on itself, it repeats itself, it returns to its own obsessions, it provides dull solutions, for it too is a creature of habit, it cannot really initiate, its routes are determined. It needs the Other. But it cannot create the Other. Whether it will meet the Other is a matter of chance. (*PM* 214)

This is a crisp summary of the interaction of heredity and the accidental that has been explored in many of Drabble's other novels. Accident is a way out of the trap of heredity; if the individual is not lucky enough to mutate into a different, more competent sort of being, then perhaps fate or luck will produce an accident to have a transforming impact on the personality. As the reader then learns, the Other, in the form of Nicolas Gaulden, enters Chrissie's life at university; he collides with her parent-patterned career, and knocks it off course. Chrissie marries Nicolas within two years, and leaves university without a degree. She feels that 'she had truly escaped Bessie at last. She had burned her boats' (*PM* 255).

The narrative is ambivalent about Nick Gaulden's impact on Chrissie's life: the word 'escape' is used here to show that she has broken free of the hereditary path, or at least of the newly established parental, educational path, but 'escape' is also used of the tie to Nick: 'If Nick had not come for her then, would she have escaped him?' (*PM* 254), for the marriage is unsuccessful. At Nicolas Gaulden's funeral, Chrissie, his first wife, counts his second wife and five mistresses, nearly all with children by him. Now married again to a charming and titled historian, Chrissie is not sure whether her life had been ruined or not; it had certainly been full of suffering, as she endured jealousy and regret, even after her divorce from Nick. Thus Nick could be seen as an avenue of escape, or as another fatal, devouring spouse, quite different from Bessie Bawtry, but also destructive; the narrator is ambivalent, as is Chrissie, on whether her gains from the passionate relationship were worth the subsequent sufferings.

Faro too, in the next generation, has her own problem of choice. Her boyfriend Sebastian is given to emotional blackmail, and Faro, who really wants to leave him, allows herself to be pressed into continuing to give him her attention; he is 'her clog and her dependant and she is sick to death of him. He has gone dead, like a spent match, like grey coke, like clinker. He is a dead weight, pulling at her, like an old sick dog' (*PM* 266). So far, then, he is like Bessie Bawtry, who had been 'a real bloodsucker, as well as a shrew' (*PM* 235). Seb fastens on to Faro just as Bessie had fastened on to Joe, and apparently Faro has inherited some of Joe's sense of responsibility, his vulnerability to emotional blackmail. In the event, Seb overplays his hand: in a parody of the ambiguous illness (clinical depression), which Bessie uses to justify her comfortable dependency and extravagant claims, Seb pretends to be suffering from cancer of the pancreas. After some concern, Faro discovers that he has been lying to her, which gives her the impetus to leave him for good. So Faro at least escapes both the pressure of the past and the bloodsucker that lay in wait for her. Chance finds its justifiable role in the scheme of things.

Like *The Gates of Ivory*, *The Peppered Moth* has a dual time-scheme, which appropriately draws out the parallels and influences of the elder generation upon the younger lives which have inherited its genes. The narrative cuts back from its prologue at the DNA lecture to Bessie Bawtry's childhood in a cramped terrace house amid the coalfields. The narrator both draws in the reader with a consistent 'we', and moves in and out of the clichéd phrasing of the typical small-town audience, seeming also to identify with the local citizens: introducing the meeting in the former chapel, the narrator asks 'Are we about to hear a sermon? ... we don't have to put up with that kind of thing these days' (*PM* 1). Still echoing the tone of the audience, the narrator gives some facts – 'it is a scientific meeting and

microbiologist Dr Robert Hawthorn is about to address his flock'
– but refuses to provide other information, whimsically
suggesting 'It's the present, or possibly even the future', and
asking who the beautiful young woman in the second row is,
instead of revealing straightaway that it is Faro, Bessie Bawtry's
granddaughter.

Surprisingly, after all the 'we's and 'you's, the organizing
narrator apologizes later in the novel for using 'I': 'I have tried –
and I apologise for that intrusive authorial "I" which I have
done my best to avoid – I have tried to understand why Joe and
Bessie married, and I have tried to invent some plausible
dialogue for them that might explain it' (*PM* 129), but within a
page the 'I' who is writing and shaping the narrative has
slipped back into the 'We' of posterity, becoming once more
merely a presenting narrator, admitting uniform bafflement
faced with the facts: 'We are left with the facts, and they are
sparse' (*PM* 130). It is at this point, about a third of the way
through the novel, that there is a full establishment of the dual
time-scheme, as the organizing narrator guides us from the birth
of Bessie's second child, Chrissie, to the present: 'We shall come
back to Chrissie and her childhood shortly, but meanwhile let us
return for a while – or rather let us leap forward in time – to
Chrissie's daughter and Bessie's granddaugher Faro, whom we
left, if you remember, in a Nonconformist chapel, in Bessie's
birthplace, Breaseborough, in the company of Bessie's sister, her
Great Aunt Dora' (*PM* 131). This point in time, which marks the
beginning of Faro's excursions up to Breaseborough, is the
'present' of the novel, the time of writing, from which the
flashbacks and narratives take their backward way.

The Faro section is limited to about thirty pages before the
narrative resumes Bessie's story, turning into her daughter
Chrissie's story; we hear that Bessie, who had dealt well with
war-time problems, becomes increasingly reclusive in the post-
war world, once these stimuli are removed. Chrissie's life is
taken to the age of 18; then there is a leap to Nicolas Gaulden's
funeral, after which the narrative fills in the gap of her early
relationship with him and how their relationship had rapidly
collapsed, leaving her to bring up Faro as a single parent,
sometimes even harbouring Nick's later mistresses and their
offspring in her home.

The afterword to the novel focuses many of the issues of narrative form that have appeared throughout Drabble's novels, particularly in those from *The Realms of Gold* onward. Drabble explains briefly how and why she has used this form of fictional biography, and her account draws attention to the ambiguity of the narrative process in all novels, though more than usually complex in this one. Drabble speaks in the Afterword as author, as her real self,[7] referring to her own actual life in the real world. She speaks of her approach and her decisions about what to put in, what to leave out, what to change. These are responsibilities of the implied author, and are often stated explicitly in the text by the organizing narrator, and it may be that the discomfort Margaret Drabble mentions in the process relates to the unity between author, as person, and implied author, as one who has used experience rather more directly than usual to make a fiction.

The Seven Sisters, Margaret Drabble's next novel, provides another version of the 'difficult mother' story, and casts additional light on the previous two novels. It seems to explore how far a woman cast in the mould of Bessie Bawtry could, even late in life, acquire the independence of Frieda Haxby. The narrator, Candida Wilton, confesses to having been, like Bessie, depressed, neurotic and given to tantrums, at least while menopausal, and she has also been frigid and unsupportive towards her charming husband Andrew. Unlike Joe Barron, Andrew does not cherish her but instead, like Frieda's husband Andrew, has an affair with another woman, which this time ends not tragically but in a civilized divorce. Thus Candida, secretly pleased to be rid of a husband she considers to be a hypocrite and a patronizing prig, accepts, though with some irritation, the humiliations of a rejected wife.

The novel begins as Candida's diary, typed like Frieda's into her computer, and telling the story of her new life. To everyone's amazement, though in her 50s and with no family, friends or work to attract her there, she has decided to move to London, and with Andrew's handsome divorce settlement has bought a spartan two-room flat on the third floor of a house in Ladbroke Grove, a run-down area on the fringe of fashionable Notting Hill. Here respectable or well-to-do inhabitants like Candida's few friends mix with a floating population of immigrants, beggars, criminals, and a variously deprived and aggressive underclass. Through both symbolism and narrative complexity, Drabble has compressed layers of further meaning into the limited parameters of Candida's existence. One of her first attempts to fill her empty life in these alien surroundings has been to join an evening class on Virgil's *Aeneid*, an old-fashioned subject, as she notes, and one which is promptly abolished as the whole adult institute is sold, gutted and turned into a health club. Along with other dispossessed students, Candida is given a cheap subscription to this expensive club, and *The Aeneid* and the health club together provide surprising new directions in her activities and development of sympathies.

Reading *The Aeneid*, Candida has identified to some extent with Dido, queen of Carthage, abandoned by the hero Aeneas so that he can pursue his destiny, go to Italy and become the founder of Rome. The abandoned Dido kills herself, and this establishes one of several hints that Candida may put an end to her lonely life by suicide. Her class had been particularly interested in book six of the story, in which Aeneas and a few companions are allowed by the Cumaean Sybil, a prophetess favoured by Apollo, to go down into the Underworld. The London streets around Ladbroke Grove are a kind of underworld to Candida, and the dirt, decay and incomprehensible signs and posters that she sees are described vividly; gradually, however, she becomes interested in shopkeepers, tramps and eccentrics, begins to speak to some of them and starts to see them as individuals rather than an undifferentiated, threatening mass.

In the health club she refuses to speak to any other members at first, a parallel to her earlier lack of concern for the pupils at her ex-husband's school. As time passes, however, in spite of her own protestations ('I don't care. I'm curious, but curiosity has nothing to do with caring', SS 110), she takes an interest in a doomed young woman with an ominous lump on her back, and tries to draw her out of her depression. Little by little the self-focused, self-pitying tone that she detects in her early diary entries is mitigated by an increase of concern, self-criticism and humour.

A windfall from a long-forgotten pension investment allows Candida to arrange an excursion with friends from her Virgil class – these are her colourful friend Anaïs, the competent Mrs Barclay, and their teacher, the sybil-like Mrs Jerrold (who foresees Candida floating like Ophelia in the water) – along with two friends from former days, her schoolfriend, popular novelist Julia Jordan, and the Suffolk social worker, Sally Hepburn. They travel to the site of Carthage at Tunis, then retrace Aeneas's journey to Italy and to the mouth of the Underworld, where Candida seems to have a vague feeling that the Cumaean Sybil and the Underworld itself will still be there and accessible to them.

In the journey part of the novel the narrative changes to the third person, and the narrator gives us a picture of Candida interacting with her friends (she behaves better than the morbid, suspicious first-person monologue has led us to expect). These six women with their tall, dynamic, Italian tour guide, Valeria, make up the seven sisters of the title. What they say about their past lives and their present state also helps Candida reflect on her own situation, and the women help each other when the unexpected crises typical of Drabble novels afflict them at the last stage of their holiday (Mrs Barclay's husband has been attacked and injured; Candida hears that her daughter Ellen is in hospital in Amsterdam).

The next section of the novel opens with the sentence 'What you and I have read so far is the story that I found on my mother's laptop, after her mysterious and unexpected death' (*SS* 251). There follows a commentary by Candida's daughter Ellen, describing her mother's apparent suicide by drowning in the canal, as prepared for by various earlier hints; she also notes the unreliability of her mother's narrative, her unfairness to her so-called friend Sally Hepburn (vilified by Candida as fat, patronizing, nosy, malicious) and the role of her frigid, uncooperative behaviour in the breakdown of her marriage. Her narcissism is also criticized, specifically in that she has never said anything about Ellen's responsible and important job as a speech therapist in a Finnish clinic.

This section is less like the multiple-narrator approach found in many modern novels and more like the duality of *The Waterfall*, where the narrative is critical of itself, for the next section reveals that Candida is still alive: 'I can't get out. I try, but I can't escape ... I'm back in the same old story' (*SS* 275). She had written the 'Ellen' part herself as an exercise in self-criticism, and her comment questions the whole process of novel-writing, the validity of all novelists' efforts to explore human consciousness: 'How impossible it is, to enter the consciousness of another person. How impossible, to escape from one's own' (SS 277). Nonetheless she had found that the Ellen persona had allowed her to think of various interpretations of her life that had never occurred to her before. This final part of the novel shows, in alternative passages of first-person and third-person narrative, that Candida is trying to change her behaviour, and repair past errors in her relationships. She painfully but regularly telephones Ellen in Finland, and has become reconciled to her youngest daughter Martha. She has come to perceive their teasing as friendly, not hostile.

Possibly Candida's journey into the underworld and the happier voyage to Italian shores has helped her to break out of a tunnel that was threatening to lead to the suicide that did not happen. The health club too leads her to spiritual health, by opening out a space for her to observe other people, as she does in more harried circumstances in the streets around Ladbroke Grove. At the end of the holiday section, there is a short sequence describing Candida's solitary expedition to the supposed site of the Cumaean Sybil's cell. Alone, she meditates and tries to commune with the Sybil's spirit. The voice of the Sybil seems to tell her to stop struggling to live: 'Be still. Submit. You can climb no higher. This is the last height. Submit'. Candida, however, is infused with some of the spirit of her creator, who had said back in 1980: 'That's what we were put on this earth to do: to endeavour in the face of the impossible', and her narrative continues 'But it is not the last height. And she cannot submit' (SS 247). This is why the crisp ending of a suicide is not for her; she has to go on. As in other Drabble novels, there is no closure: Candida waits for her destiny, but with a sense that it is a continuing journey.

Margaret Drabble's latest novel to date, The Red Queen, probes again the slippage between real author and implied author, and the uncertainty of presenting and interpreting events in the past. In a prologue and afterword she explains the genesis of the novel, which is based on the memoirs of an eighteenth-century Korean crown princess (variously known as Princess Hong or Lady Hyegyong). Drabble explains that she found the story of this strong-minded woman irresistible, and, feeling that she was being directed by her insistent subject made the memoirs into a novel. The first half of the novel gives the dramatic history of the crown princess's marriage to the oppressed and eventually mad and murderous Crown Prince Sado, and the second half describes the memoir's impact on a modern fictional character Barbara Halliwell. This is not an interwoven dual time-scheme like that of *The Gates of Ivory* or *The Peppered Moth*, but the two periods, 200 years apart, are compared and contrasted at intervals, and Drabble boldly asserts what she notes is a heresy against postmodern orthodoxy, namely that the crown princess's personality appeals to the reader as an example of universal human spirit.

The prologue and afterword, then, spell out the author's intentions at least as far as the theme of transcultural identity is concerned. The first part of the novel is narrated in the first person by the crown princess herself, but not merely as another version of her existing, historic memoirs. The events of two centuries ago are being narrated now by the surviving, disembodied spirit of the crown princess, and we are asked to see her as inhabiting a posthumous state in which she reads books and newspapers, and even dabbles with the internet although she cannot interact with living people except by mental pressure. Thus in this version of her life story she can marshal the modern psychological theories she has read about, and make pertinent comparisons with later social history. She is not however able to see hidden events or personal motives, so her account remains, as the real author in the prologue says merely one of the many possible interpretations of the past.

The second part of the novel has a third-person narrator of limited omniscience describing the experiences and thoughts of Dr Barbara Halliwell but not the inner thoughts of other characters; sometimes, however, as in *The Peppered Moth*, the narrator fixes the observing position as 'we', and the reader is drawn in as a member of a chorus of observers or 'spies', hovering near Barbara Halliwell like the sylphs in Pope's *The Rape of the Lock*. As in Dickens's *Bleak House*, the crown princess's first-person narrative is in the past tense, and the third-person narrative is in the present tense. The style too differs, as the crown princess's account is cautious and spare, whereas Barbara's experiences are built up from a wealth of specific detail as in Drabble's earlier novels.

As well as this layering of real author and two narrators, Margaret Drabble introduces herself as a character in the novel appearing in a cameo role, meeting and befriending Dr Halliwell in the final pages as a transition to the framing situation in which she becomes the writer of the novel about the crown princess and Babs Halliwell. Self-referentially, then, the production of the novel itself is the culmination of the crown princess's ghostly campaign, as she seeks for the meaning of her unique place in history; she wants her story to be more and more widely known, so that she will be helped to make sense of her life. In *The Waterfall*, Jane Gray had believed that she would receive perfect enlightenment at the moment of death: the crown princess, who exists beyond her own death and has not been enlightened, believes that at the end of time we shall see the universal and know all things. But she hopes to piece together some kind of understanding before that, with the assistance of her living 'ghosts'.

The selection of Barbara Halliwell as an envoy into the modern world is partly due to coincidence, and the interest in chance, accident and coincidence is strong enough in Barbara's life to suggest that coincidence and chance are the only explanations available. For example, coincidentally, the crown princess, Barbara Halliwell and Margaret Drabble are united by a strong attraction towards the colour red, and the crown princess's childhood longing for a red silk skirt was what appealed to her 'envoys'. On a more serious level, when Dr Halliwell reads the memoirs she is on the way to give a paper on 'Dying by Lot: Uncertainty and Fatality' at a conference in Korea. Her interest both in accident and in the memoirs is prompted by the death of her only child, many years before, as a toddler, from a rare immune deficiency disease of which Barbara was unknowingly a carrier, possibly hastened by her consent to ineffective and ultimately fatal medication. The crown princess also lost her first child to a wasting disease which could have been due to some kind of immune deficiency. A further coincidence appears in their married lives: Crown Prince Sado had been bullied by his royal father, and developed a form of madness which began in a clothes fetishism and blossomed into a series of murders of court ladies, eunuchs, ordinary citizens and his favourite mistress. The crown princess escaped with having a heavy chessboard thrown at her face. Babs's husband also developed depression evolving into suicidal madness, possibly because of pressure from his overbearing father, and though he had no clothes fetish, and had not murdered anyone, he had tried to strangle Babs during a quarrel. The crown prince had been forced by his father into a gruesome death by starvation, locked up in a large rice-chest. Babs's husband remains enclosed in a living death of heavy medication and immobility in an institution.

The novel is subtitled *A Transcultural Tragicomedy*, and Barbara's section of the novel includes its own accidents and coincidences, often comic in nature. Her seizing of the wrong suitcase at the Korean airport leads to friendship with its owner, Dr Oo, a medical doctor attending a parallel conference, who escorts her round some sites associated with the crown princess. Barbara also has a three-day love affair with the ageing but charismatic Jan Van Jost, star of the conference, a romance initiated by her telling him of the fascinating memoirs of the crown princess. As in so many Drabble novels, there is a shocking catastrophe, when Van Jost dies of a heart attack while in bed with Barbara. (Neat plotting means that Dr Oo is available to support Barbara in this crisis.) This in turn leads to Barbara's eventually contacting Van Jost's young third wife, on whose behalf he had been trying to adopt a Chinese orphan. In the final section, Barbara and Van Jost's widow find the little Chinese girl and bring her to Van Jost's home in Spain, from which she visits Barbara in England. The child seems in a way to balance the loss of the infants of the crown princess and Barbara. The spirit of the crown princess sees her as a new envoy of her life.

Barbara Halliwell, as a capable independent woman who pursues meaning amid a confused mass of accidents and repeated motifs, has something in common with earlier Drabble heroines Frances Wingate and Kate Armstrong. In *The Middle Ground*, Kate went back to her native Romley and walked along the buried sewage pipe, recalling buried memories of her childhood. Similarly, Barbara walks along an overgrown ravine near her London home, a wasteland marginalized by new roads, flyovers and underpasses: the ravine path reminds her of the ravine in the crown princess's palace garden and represents for her, as for Kate, the strange relationship of past and present –

112

reflective, contiguous, but never united. There is no sudden insight for Kate or Barbara, but both develop the gradual sense that the past must be integrated with new pursuits and that the lessons of the past can only be applied by living more actively. Once more the continuing journey opens before the ghost and her ghost writers.

9

Conclusion

Looking at the structure and narrative approach of Margaret Drabble's novels, it is clear that her interest in determinism, free will, heredity, upbringing and accident have caused her novels to include significant amounts of retrospective narrative, accidents and coincidences, and explanatory narrative interventions. As she says, within the novels and in life, there is conflict:

> Fate and character are irreconcilable. That's why I write the books. The whole point of writing a novel, for me, is to try to work out the balance between these two, and there is no answer ... I'm not sure that character is wholly fate in that one is moulded by certain elements. Yes, I suppose that's a kind of Freudian predeterminism; I do believe in that kind of predeterminism. But I also believe in the possibility of accident because anyone with any common sense must believe in accident. I suppose I'm trying to do what one has to do in life, to reconcile the importance of fate, the destiny, the character and the accidents that hit you on the way.[1]

but she admits that she doesn't use the word 'fate' with any constant meaning.[2]

In the novels, the narrative presents the interplay of these concerns and shows the shifting balance between them, by depicting characters determined by their genetic legacy, their upbringing, trying to exert their will, and afflicted by accidents. Drabble pays attention to the effects of family, in terms of heritage and upbringing, and, as she says, tends to do this by looking back at the past rather than proceeding step by step, chronologically from childhood to adulthood. This means that the reminiscences of the past can be introduced either where the implied author thinks convenient, or as part of the characters' own discovery of themselves. This is especially significant when a character looks back into the past and discovers memories which have been repressed, never thought about for many years.

The arrangement of past material, including explanations of upbringing and other influences, and of challenging accidents, results in the shape of the plot. Margaret Drabble is ambivalent about the amount of conscious control she gives to her novels:

> What's technique for, except to do something with, not an end in itself ... I think structure is the support of what is being done and said ... Anybody can make a space; it's the shape of it and what's in it that's interesting, I think. You can impose a structure on anything. It is to create a natural structure that looks natural, that looks organic, that's difficult and that's worth doing. So it's got to look organic, it's got to look as if it's part of the body of the work.[3]

But immediately afterwards, speaking of structural devices, which should never be obtrusive, she adds 'Also I'm sure that in some of them I don't know what I'm doing and I'm quite often surprised when I re-read something to see how it's made because I never plan these things; they just occur, or don't occur as the case may be'.[4] Though this may apply only to specific structural devices, Drabble says that she also does not plan her novels in advance; of *The Radiant Way*, she says 'I knew the subject matter but not the incident or the plot' and, although she had an idea of the ending (the picnic in the country), she disclaims any working towards a climax – 'the end is only a mood, isn't it?'[5]

The effect of the arrangement of the material in the narrative is clearly different; Clara's background is established in a large section at the beginning of the novel, so that thereafter the reader follows her progress with a strong sense of the influences which have shaped her and which she is trying to escape; the insight into her own mother's past comes too late for her to sympathize, and hints at the way the past has already affected Clara too. By contrast, Liz Headleand's past life is explained in short reminiscences spread throughout the narrative, and subject to her own expert scrutiny and reinterpretation, with the unknown material being revealed at intervals among the familiar memories.

Unlike the conventional crime story, the revelations from the past are not simple answers to questions, but require new understanding and changed readings. Drabble looks at her approach in the light of the theory of biography studies, referred to by her husband Michael Holroyd, the biographer – 'he says that our lives are built on a sequence of what you would call inventions about what you think had happened'.[6] Changes to vital information about one's past mean 'that one would be in a different story. But it would be a completely retrospective different story. The whole of one's life would be exactly the same in every detail, simply that one would have to rewrite the plot'.[7] This in effect is what Jane Gray is trying to do, at the end of *The Waterfall*, but other characters also find themselves rethinking their ideas of themselves and other people.

The impression taken from Drabble's work, then, is not of traditional realist novels about interesting people, but one of uncertain, doubtfully motivated characters, discovering and remaking themselves, reorganizing their previous certainties into new uncertainties, in the constant interaction of past with new experiences. For some the hand of the past lies more heavily on their behaviour; for others interpretation leads to greater freedom.

Notes

CHAPTER 1. MARGARET DRABBLE: CAREER AND CRITICS

1. Olga Kenyon (ed.), *Women Writers Talk: Interviews with Ten Women Writers* (Oxford: Lennard Publishing, 1989), 37.
2. Gillian Parker and Janet Todd, 'Margaret Drabble', in Janet Todd (ed.), *Women Writers Talking* (New York: Holmes and Meier, 1983), 161–78 (p. 172).
3. See Valerie Grosvenor Myer's systematic tracing of literary allusions in Drabble's novels, in her *Margaret Drabble: A Reader's Guide* (New York: St Martin's Press; London: Vision Press, 1991).
4. For instance in Dee Preussner, 'Talking with Margaret Drabble', *Modern Fiction Studies*, 25 (Winter 1979–80), 563–77 (p. 571).
5. Iris Rozencwajg, 'Interview with Margaret Drabble', *Women's Studies*, 6 (1979), 335–47, 346.
6. This is a case of life *not* imitating art, as Drabble could be seen as making the opposite decision compared with her heroine Emma in *The Garrick Year*, published two years earlier.
7. Joanne Creighton, *Margaret Drabble* (London: Methuen, 1985), 9.
8. Dee Preussner, 'Patterns in the Garrick Year', in Dory Schmidt (ed.), *Margaret Drabble: Golden Realms* (Edinburg, TX: Pan American University, 1982), 117–27 (p. 117).
9. Myer, 59.
10. Lynn Veach Sadler, *Margaret Drabble* (Boston: Twayne, 1986), 3.
11. Ibid., Introduction, i.
12. Jita Tuzyline Allan, *Womanist and Feminist Aesthetics: A Comparative Review* (Athens, OH: Ohio University Press, 1995), 46.
13. Ibid., 47.
14. Drabble points out that 'there was no feminist criticism around' when she started writing (Parker and Todd, 166).
15. Diana Cooper-Clark, 'Margaret Drabble: Cautious Feminist', *Atlantic Monthly* , 247 (November 1980), 69–75 (p. 70).
16. Ibid., 75.

17. Nicole Suzanne Bokat, *The Novels of Margaret Drabble: 'This Freudian Family Nexus'* (New York: Peter Lang, 1998), 2.
18. Preussner, 571.
19. Parker and Todd, 171.
20. Confirmed in conversation with the present writer.
21. Nancy S. Hardin, 'An Interview with Margaret Drabble', *Contemporary Literature*, 14 (Summer 1973), 273–95 (p. 277).
22. Allan, 51.
23. Hardin, 293.
24. For example, in Hardin, 286.
25. Fumi Takano, *Margaret Drabble in Tokyo* (Tokyo: Kenkyusha, 1991), 5.
26. Margaret Drabble, in conversation with Glenda Leeming, 10 July 2002. Henceforth, Drabble in conversation with Leeming.
27. Takano, 11.
28. Ibid.
29. For instance, Adam Mars Jones, as late as 2001, reviewing *The Peppered Moth*, in the *Observer*, 7 January 2001.
30. Myer, 141.
31. Takano, 20.
32. Drabble in conversation with Leeming.
33. Hardin, 278.
34. Rosencwajg, 339.

CHAPTER 2. NARRATIVE STRUCTURE IN DRABBLE'S WORKS

1. Some definitions of narrative extend it to any statement, however short, which implies a sequence of events, but for the purposes of this discussion I am taking a narrower definition.
2. For example, Robert Merrill notes that 'we still use the term *plot* in a highly limited, almost pejorative sense, referring exclusively to a work's external events or narrative sequence ... [but] plot is not simply a sequence of events, but such a sequence shaped for a particular end or purpose' ('Raymond Chandler's Plots and the Concept of Plot', *Narrative*, 7, (January 1999), 3–21 (pp. 3–4).
3. For instance, Peter Brooks: 'narratives work on us, as readers, to create models of understanding ... we need and want such shaping orders' (*Reading for the Plot*, New York: Knopf Press, 1984, xiii).
4. Cooper-Clark, 75.
5. Barbara Milton, 'An Interview with Margaret Drabble', *Paris Review*, 20 (Fall–Winter 1978), 40–65 (p. 43).

6. Ibid., 62.
7. John Hannay, 'Margaret Drabble: An Interview', *Twentieth Century Literature*, 33 (1987), 129–48 (p. 139).
8. Hardin, 283.
9. Cooper-Clark, 73.
10. Creighton, 'An Interview with Margaret Drabble', in Dorey Schmidt, *Margaret Drabble: Golden Realms* (Edinburg, TX: Pan American University Press, 1980), 18–31 (p. 18).
11. I shall refer to the narrator as if of the same gender as the author, unless it is clearly not the case.
12. Hardin, 292.
13. Drabble, in conversation with Leeming, 10 July 2002.
14. Mieke Bal, *Narratology: Introduction to the Theory of Narrative*, trans. Christine van Boheeman (Toronto: University of Toronto Press, 1985), 119.
15. Bal possibly undermines this interpretative position by her reference to the reader: 'No matter how absurd, tangled or unreal a text may be, readers will tend to regard what they consider as "normal" as a criterion by which they can give meaning to a text' (ibid., 12).
16. Drabble, in conversation with Leeming, 10 July 2002.
17. Quoted in Wolfgang Iser, *Prospecting: From Reader Response to Literary Anthropology* (Baltimore: Johns Hopkins University Press, 1989), 57.
18. Ibid., 63.
19. Hardin, 293–4.

CHAPTER 3. SPOTS OF TIME: MANAGING A FOCUSED NARRATIVE

1. Rozencwajg, 343.
2. Milton, 45.
3. Kenyon, 38.
4. Cooper-Clark, 74–5.
5. Rozencwajg, 343.
6. Milton, 57.
7. Parker and Todd, 170.
8. The affair of Susie Enderby in *A Natural Curiosity* is a case in point.
9. Cooper-Clark, 70.
10. Hardin, 281.
11. Drabble in conversation with Leeming.
12. Milton, 44.

13. Parker and Todd, 168.
14. Drabble in conversation with Leeming.
15. Valerie Grosvenor Myer has also noted these and other Words-worthian echoes in the novels in her *Margaret Drabble: A Reader's Guide.*
16. Cooper-Clark, 70.

CHAPTER 4. AN EVENT SEEN FROM AN ANGLE

1. Cooper-Clark, 72.
2. Rozencwajg, 338.
3. Parker and Todd, 166.
4. Creighton, in Schmidt, 23.
5. Hardin, 293.

CHAPTER 5. WHAT WAS THE POINT OF KNOWING WHAT WAS RIGHT (IF ONE DIDN'T THEN DO IT)?

1. Takano, 96.
2. Parker and Todd, 168.
3. Creighton, in Schmidt, 23.
4. Hardin, 294.

CHAPTER 6. I DO NOT CARE VERY MUCH FOR PLOTS MYSELF (BUT I DO LIKE A SEQUENCE OF EVENTS)

1. Takano, 13.
2. Parker and Todd, in Todd, 167.
3. Wordsworth, 'The Old Cumberland Beggar'.
4. Drabble refers to Arthur Koestler's *The Roots of Coincidence* (London: Hutchinson, 1972) which puts forward this view; e.g. on p. 86.
5. Cooper-Clark, 75.
6. Parker and Todd, 176–7.
7. Cooper-Clark, 75.
8. The director is Gabriel Denham, last seen as Clara's lover in *Jerusalem the Golden.*

CHAPTER 7. READING THE PLOT OF THE PAST

1. Kenyon, 37.
2. Ibid., 36
3. Ibid., 33–4. Drabble emphasizes that 'These questions are quite serious; they are not, or not only, a rhetorical device' (in Takano, 17).

CHAPTER 8. MOTHERS AND OTHERS

1. Drabble in conversation with Leeming.
2. Takano, 22.
3. Ibid., 46.
4. The term is taken from philosopher John Rawl's *A Theory of Justice* (Oxford: Oxford University Press, 1972), cited by Drabble in *Case for Equality* (see note 5 below).
5. Drabble in conversation with Leeming. She delivered a speech on the subject to the Progressive League on 22 April 1988, published as *Case for Equality: Fabian Tract 527* (London: Fabian Society, 1988).
6. Drabble in conversation with Leeming.
7. Drabble in conversation with Leeming.

CHAPTER 9. CONCLUSION

1. Preussner, 56–7.
2. Hannay, 'Interview', 147.
3. Creighton, 27.
4. Ibid.
5. Kenyon, 33.
6. Hannay, 'Interview', 140.
7. Ibid., 139.

Select Bibliography

BIBLIOGRAPHY

Packer, Joan Garrett, *Margaret Drabble: An Annotated Bibliography* (New York: Garland, 1988).

Soule, George, *Four British Women Novelists: Anita Brookner, Margaret Drabble, Iris Murdoch, Barbara Pym – An Annotated and Critical Secondary Bibliography* (Lanham, MD, and London: Scarecrow Press; and Pasadena and Englewood Cliffs: Salem Press, 1998).

WORKS BY MARGARET DRABBLE

Novels

A Summer Bird-Cage (London: Weidenfeld & Nicolson, 1962; reissued Harmondsworth, Penguin, 1963).

The Garrick Year (London: Weidenfeld & Nicolson, 1964; reissued Harmondsworth, Penguin, 1966).

The Millstone (London: Weidenfeld & Nicolson, 1965; reissued Harmondsworth, Penguin, 1968).

Jerusalem the Golden (London: Weidenfeld & Nicolson, 1967; reissued Harmondsworth, Penguin, 1969).

The Waterfall (London: Weidenfeld & Nicolson, 1969; reissued Harmondsworth, Penguin, 1971).

The Needle's Eye (London: Weidenfeld & Nicolson, 1972; reissued Harmondsworth, Penguin, 1973).

The Realms of Gold (London: Weidenfeld & Nicolson, 1975; reissued Harmondsworth, Penguin, 1977).

The Ice Age (London: Weidenfeld & Nicolson, 1977; reissued Harmondsworth, Penguin, 1978).

The Middle Ground (London: Weidenfeld & Nicolson, 1980; reissued Harmondsworth, Penguin, 1982)

The Radiant Way (London: Weidenfeld & Nicolson, 1987; reissued Harmondsworth, Penguin, 1988).

A Natural Curiosity (London: Viking, 1989; reissued Harmondsworth, Penguin, 1990).

The Gates of Ivory (London: Viking, 1991; reissued Harmondsworth, Penguin, 1992).

The Witch of Exmoor (London: Viking, 1996; reissued Harmondsworth, Penguin, 1997).

The Peppered Moth (London: Viking, 2000; reissued Harmondsworth: Penguin, 2001).

The Seven Sisters (London: Viking, 2002; reissued Harmondsworth: Penguin, 2003).

The Red Queen (London: Viking, 2004).

Short stories

'Les Liaisons Dangereuses', *Punch*, 247 (28 October 1964), 646–8.

'Hassan's Tower', in *Winter's Tales 12*, ed. A. B. Maclean (London: Macmillan; New York: St Martin's Press, 1966), 149–68.

'A Voyage to Cythera' *Mademoiselle*, 66 (December 1967), 98–9,148–50.

'The Reunion', in *Winter's Tales 14*, ed. Kevin Crossley-Holland (London: Macmillan; New York: St Martin's Press, 1968), 149–68.

'Faithful Lovers', *Saturday Evening Post*, 241 (6 April 1968), 62, 64–5.

'A Pyrrhic Victory', *Nova*, July 1968, 80, 84, 86.

'Crossing the Alps', in *Penguin Modern Stories*, 3, ed. Judith Burnley (London: Penguin, 1969), 63–84; repr. in *Mademoiselle*, 72 (February 1971), 154–5, 193–8.

'The Gifts of War', in *Winter's Tales 16*, ed. A. B. Maclean (London: Macmillan; New York: St Martin's Press, 1970), 20–26; repr. in *Women and Fiction: Short Stories By and About Women*, ed. Susan Cahill (New York: New American Library, 1975), 335–47.

'A Day in the Life of a Smiling Woman', *Cosmopolitan* (October 1973), 224, 252–7; repr. in *In the Looking Glass: Twenty-One Modern Short Stories by Women*, ed. Nancy Dean and Myra Stark (New York: Putnam, 1977), 143–65.

'A Success Story', *Spare Rib*, London, 1973; *Ms.*, 3 (December 1974), 53–5, 94; repr. in *Fine Lines: The Best of Ms. Fiction*, ed. Ruth Sullivan (New York: Scribners, 1982), 259–71.

'Homework', *Cosmopolitan*, November 1975, 192–8; repr. in *Ontario Review*, 7 (1977–8), 7–13.

'The Dying Year', *Harper's Magazine*, July 1987, 59–69.

Other works

Arnold Bennett, a Biography (London: Weidenfeld & Nicolson, 1974; reissued London: Futura Publications, 1975).
The Genius of Thomas Hardy (London: Weidenfeld & Nicolson, 1976).
For Queen and Country: Britain in the Victorian Age (London: André Deutsch, 1978).
A Writer's Britain (London: Thames and Hudson, 1979).
Case for Equality: Fabian Society Tract 527 (London: Fabian Society, 1988).
Angus Wilson, a Biography (London: Secker and Warburg, 1995).
The Oxford Companion to English Literature (Oxford: Oxford University Press, 1985; 2nd edn. 2000).

Interviews

Cooper-Clark, Diana, 'Margaret Drabble: Cautious Feminist', *Atlantic Monthly*, 247 (November 1980), 69–75; repr. in Ellen Cronan Rose (ed.), *Critical Essays on Margaret Drabble* (Boston: G. K. Hall, 1985).
Creighton, Joanne V., 'An Interview with Margaret Drabble', in Dorey Schmidt (ed.), *Margaret Drabble: Golden Realms* (Edinburg, TX: Pan American University, 1982).
Fox-Genovese, Elizabeth, 'The Ambiguities of Female Identity: A Reading of the Novels of Margaret Drabble', *Partisan Review*, 46 (1979), 234–48.
Hannay, John, 'Margaret Drabble: An Interview', *Twentieth Century Literature*, 33 (1987), 129–48.
Hardin, Nancy S., 'An Interview with Margaret Drabble', *Contemporary Literature*, 14 (Summer 1973), 273–95.
Kenyon, Olga, *Women Writers Talk: Interviews with Ten Women Writers* (Oxford: Lennard Publishing, 1989; New York: Carroll & Graf, 1990).
Milton, Barbara, 'An Interview with Margaret Drabble', *Paris Review*, 20 (Fall–Winter 1978), 40–65.
Parker, Gillian, and Janet Todd, 'Margaret Drabble', in Janet Todd (ed.), *Women Writers Talking* (New York: Holmes and Meier, 1983), 161–78.
Pickering, Jean, 'Margaret Drabble's Sense of the Middle Problem', *Twentieth Century Literature*, 30 (Winter 1984), 475–83.
Preussner, Dee, 'Talking with Margaret Drabble', *Modern Fiction Studies*, 25 (Winter 1979), 563–77.
Rozencwajg, Iris, 'Interview with Margaret Drabble', *Women's Studies*, 6 (1979), 335–47.

CRITICAL WORKS

Allan, Tuzyline Jita, *Womanist and Feminist Aesthetics: A Comparative Review* (Athens, OH: Ohio University Press, 1995). An example of the unfavourable kind of feminist viewpoint that Drabble sometimes mentions.

Bal, Mieke, *Narratology: Introduction to the Theory of Narrative*, trans. Christine van Boheeman (Toronto: University of Toronto Press, 1985). As background to narratology studies, significant introduction to different narrative approaches.

Bokat, Nicole Suzanne, *The Novels of Margaret Drabble: 'This Freudian Family Nexus'* (New York: Peter Lang, 1998). Rather narrowly focused psychological analysis.

Bramberg, Pamela S., 'Narrative in Drabble's *The Middle Ground*: Relativity versus Teleology', *Contemporary Literature*, 24 (Winter 1983), 463–79. Useful in emphasising the postmodern aspect of Drabble's work.

Brooks, Peter, *Reading for the Plot* (New York: Knopf Press, 1984). As background reading to narrative theory, survey of the importance of narrative techniques.

Campbell, Jane, 'Reacting Outwards: Versions of Reality in *The Middle Ground*', *Journal of Narrative Technique*, 14 (Winter 1984), 17–32. A corrective view of Drabble's presentation of subjective interpretations of the world.

Creighton, Joanne V., *Margaret Drabble* (London: Methuen, 1985). Usefully discusses Drabble's work up to *The Middle Ground*, pointing to new development of scope and technique.

Gullette, Margaret Morgenroth, *Safe at Last in the Middle Years: The Invention of the Midlife Progress Novel: Saul Bellow, Margaret Drabble, Ann Tyler, John Updike* (Berkeley: University of California Press, 1988). Places *The Middle Ground* in context of novels on similar topics.

Hannay, John, *The Intertextuality of Fate: A Study of Margaret Drabble* (Columbia: University of Missouri Press, 1986). Extensive discussion of fate in the novels, as related to poetic justice, inevitability and Providence.

Iser, Wolfgang, *Prospecting: From Reader Response to Literary Anthropology* (Baltimore: Johns Hopkins University Press, 1989). Background to aspects of narrative; essays on modern critical views.

Kenyon, Olga, *Women Novelists Today: A Survey of English Writing in the Seventies and Eighties* (New York: St Martin's Press, 1988). Short view of Drabble in the context of her contemporaries.

Moran, Mary Hurley, *Margaret Drabble: Existing within Structures* (Carbondale: Southern Illinois University Press, 1983). Mainly discusses themes and social pressures.

Myer, Valerie Grosvenor, *Margaret Drabble: Puritanism and Permissiveness* (New York: Barnes and Noble Books, 1974). Detailed and helpful examination of Drabble's assumptions and background.

—— *Margaret Drabble: A Reader's Guide* (New York: St Martin's Press; London: Vision Press, 1991). Very useful analysis of the novels, taking in influences and references of many kinds.

Rubenstein, Roberta, 'Fragmented Bodies/Selves/Narratives: Margaret Drabble's Postmodern Turn', *Contemporary Literature*, 35 (Spring 1994), 136–55. Discusses some examples of Drabble's experiments with new forms and topics.

Sadler, Lynn Veach, *Margaret Drabble* (Boston: Twayne, 1986). A limited study which tends to find stereotypes in the novels.

Schmidt, Dorey (ed.), *Margaret Drabble: Golden Realms* (Edinburg, TX: Pan American University Press, 1982). Very helpful collection of essays on different aspects of various Drabble novels.

Showalter, Elaine, *A Literature of Their Own: British Women Novelists from Bronte to Lessing* (Princeton, NJ: Princeton University Press, 1977). Focuses on feminist issues in early Drabble novels.

Stovel, Nora, *Margaret Drabble, Symbolic Moralist* (Washington, DC: Starmont House, 1989). Analyses the novels to define their moral themes.

Takano, Fumi (ed.), *Margaret Drabble in Tokyo* (Tokyo: Kenkyusha, 1991). Interesting collection of a public lecture and an interview by Drabble set alongside a description of a Japanese woman novelist's working life.

Waugh, Patricia, *Feminine Fictions: Revisiting the Postmodern* (London: Routledge, 1989). Emphasises the modern techniques used in Drabble's novels.

Index

127

Recent and
Forthcoming Titles
in the
New Series of

WRITERS AND
THEIR WORK

WRITERS AND THEIR WORK

RECENT & FORTHCOMING TITLES

RECENT & FORTHCOMING TITLES

Title	Author
William Golding 2/e	*Kevin McCarron*
Graham Greene	*Peter Mudford*
Neil M. Gunn	*J. B. Pick*
Ivor Gurney	*John Lucas*
Hamlet 2/e	*Ann Thompson & Neil Taylor*
Thomas Hardy 2/e	*Peter Widdowson*
Tony Harrison	*Joe Kelleher*
William Hazlitt	*J. B. Priestley; R. L. Brett (intro. by Michael Foot)*
Seamus Heaney 2/e	*Andrew Murphy*
George Herbert	*T.S. Eliot (intro. by Peter Porter)*
Geoffrey Hill	*Andrew Roberts*
Gerard Manley Hopkins	*Daniel Brown*
Henrik Ibsen 2/e	*Sally Ledger*
Kazuo Ishiguro 2/e	*Cynthia Wong*
Henry James – The Later Writing	*Barbara Hardy*
James Joyce 2/e	*Steven Connor*
Julius Caesar	*Mary Hamer*
Franz Kafka	*Michael Wood*
John Keats	*Kelvin Everest*
James Kelman	*Gustav Klaus*
Hanif Kureishi	*Ruvani Ranasinha*
Samuel Johnson	*Liz Bellamy*
William Langland: *Piers Plowman*	*Claire Marshall*
King Lear	*Terence Hawkes*
Philip Larkin 2/e	*Laurence Lerner*
D. H. Lawrence	*Linda Ruth Williams*
Doris Lessing	*Elizabeth Maslen*
C. S. Lewis	*William Gray*
Wyndham Lewis and Modernism	*Andrzej Gasiorak*
David Lodge	*Bernard Bergonzi*
Katherine Mansfield	*Andrew Bennett*
Christopher Marlowe	*Thomas Healy*
Andrew Marvell	*Annabel Patterson*
Ian McEwan 2/e	*Kiernan Ryan*
Measure for Measure	*Kate Chedgzoy*
The Merchant of Venice	*Warren Chernaik*
A Midsummer Night's Dream	*Helen Hackett*
Alice Munro	*Ailsa Cox*
Vladimir Nabokov	*Neil Cornwell*
V. S. Naipaul	*Suman Gupta*
Grace Nichols	*Sarah Lawson-Welsh*
Edna O'Brien	*Amanda Greenwood*
Flann O'Brien	*Joe Brooker*
Ben Okri	*Robert Fraser*
George Orwell	*Douglas Kerr*
Othello	*Emma Smith*
Walter Pater	*Laurel Brake*
Brian Patten	*Linda Cookson*
Caryl Phillips	*Helen Thomas*
Harold Pinter	*Mark Batty*
Sylvia Plath 2/e	*Elisabeth Bronfen*
Pope Amongst the Satirists	*Brean Hammond*

RECENT & FORTHCOMING TITLES

Title	Author
Revenge Tragedies of the Renaissance	*Janet Clare*
Jean Rhys 2/e	*Helen Carr*
Richard II	*Margaret Healy*
Richard III	*Edward Burns*
Dorothy Richardson	*Carol Watts*
John Wilmot, Earl of Rochester	*Germaine Greer*
Romeo and Juliet	*Sasha Roberts*
Christina Rossetti	*Kathryn Burlinson*
Salman Rushdie 2/e	*Damian Grant*
Paul Scott	*Jacqueline Banerjee*
The Sensation Novel	*Lyn Pykett*
P. B. Shelley	*Paul Hamilton*
Sir Walter Scott	*Harriet Harvey Wood*
Iain Sinclair	*Robert Sheppard*
Christopher Smart	*Neil Curry*
Wole Soyinka	*Mpalive Msiska*
Muriel Spark	*Brian Cheyette*
Edmund Spenser	*Colin Burrow*
Gertrude Stein	*Nicola Shaughnessy*
Laurence Sterne	*Manfred Pfister*
Bram Stoker	*Andrew Maunder*
Graham Swift	*Peter Widdowson*
Jonathan Swift	*Ian Higgins*
Swinburne	*Catherine Maxwell*
Alfred Tennyson	*Seamus Perry*
W. M. Thackeray	*Richard Salmon*
D. M. Thomas	*Bran Nicol*
J. R. R. Tolkien	*Charles Moseley*
Leo Tolstoy	*John Bayley*
Charles Tomlinson	*Tim Clark*
Anthony Trollope	*Andrew Sanders*
Victorian Quest Romance	*Robert Fraser*
Marina Warner	*Laurence Coupe*
Irvine Welsh	*Berthold Schoene*
Edith Wharton	*Janet Beer*
Oscar Wilde	*Alexandra Warrick*
Angus Wilson	*Peter Conradi*
Mary Wollstonecraft	*Jane Moore*
Women's Gothic 2/e	*E. J. Clery*
Women Poets of the 19th Century	*Emma Mason*
Women Romantic Poets	*Anne Janowitz*
Women Writers of the 17th Century	*Ramona Wray*
Virginia Woolf 2/e	*Laura Marcus*
Working Class Fiction	*Ian Haywood*
W. B. Yeats	*Edward Larrissy*
Charlotte Yonge	*Alethea Hayter*

TITLES IN PREPARATION

Title	Author
Fleur Adcock	*Janet Wilson*
Ama Ata Aidoo	*Nana Wilson-Tagoe*
Matthew Arnold	*Kate Campbell*
Margaret Atwood	*Marion Wynne-Davies*
John Banville	*Peter Dempsey*
William Barnes	*Christopher Ricks*
Black British Writers	*Deidre Osborne*
William Blake	*Steven Vine*
Charlotte Brontë	*Stevie Davies*
Robert Browning	*John Woodford*
Basil Bunting	*Martin Stannard*
John Bunyan	*Tamsin Spargoe*
Children's Writers of the 19th Century	*Mary Sebag-Montefiore*
Coriolanus	*Anita Pacheco*
Cymbeline	*Peter Swaab*
Douglas Dunn	*David Kennedy*
David Edgar	*Peter Boxall*
T. S. Eliot	*Colin MacCabe*
J. G. Farrell	*John McLeod*
Nadine Gordimer	*Lewis Nkosi*
Geoffrey Grigson	*R. M. Healey*
David Hare	*Jeremy Ridgman*
Ted Hughes	*Susan Bassnett*
The Imagist Poets	*Andrew Thacker*
Ben Jonson	*Anthony Johnson*
A. L. Kennedy	*Dorothy McMillan*
Jack Kerouac	*Michael Hrebebiak*
Jamaica Kincaid	*Susheila Nasta*
Rudyard Kipling	*Jan Montefiore*
Rosamond Lehmann	*Judy Simon*
Una Marson & Louise Bennett	*Alison Donnell*
Norman MacCaig	*Alasdair Macrae*
Thomas Middleton	*Hutchings & Bromham*
John Milton	*Nigel Smith*
Much Ado About Nothing	*John Wilders*
R. K. Narayan	*Shirley Chew*
New Woman Writers	*Marion Shaw/Lyssa Randolph*
Ngugi wa Thiong'o	*Brendon Nicholls*
Religious Poets of the 17th Century	*Helen Wilcox*
Samuel Richardson	*David Deeming*
Olive Schreiner	*Carolyn Burdett*
Sam Selvon	*Ramchand & Salick*
Olive Senior	*Denise de Canes Narain*
Mary Shelley	*Catherine Sharrock*
Charlotte Smith & Helen Williams	*Angela Keane*
Ian Crichton Smith	*Colin Nicholson*
R. L. Stevenson	*David Robb*
Tom Stoppard	*Nicholas Cadden*
Elizabeth Taylor	*N. R. Reeve*
Dylan Thomas	*Chris Wiggington*
Three Avant-Garde Poets	*Peter Middleton*
Three Lyric Poets	*William Rowe*

TITLES IN PREPARATION

Title	Author
Derek Walcott	*Stephen Regan*
Jeanette Winterson	*Gina Vitello*
Women's Poetry at the Fin de Siècle	*Anna Vadillo*
William Wordsworth	*Nicola Trott*